Science Up to Standards

Grades 5-8

by
Pam Walker and Elaine Wood

Cover Design
by
Matthew Van Zomeren

Inside Illustrations
by
Janet Armbrust

Published by Instructional Fair • TS Denison
an imprint of

 McGraw-Hill
Children's Publishing

About the Authors

Pam Walker and Elaine Wood currently teach biology and chemistry at Alexander High School in Douglasville, Georgia. Both authors are active in Project Wild and Project Learning Tree, conservation groups in which they interact with students of all ages. Pam and Elaine have been co-authoring books for several years. Their list of published books includes five teacher resource books and two textbooks.

Credits

Authors: Pam Walker and Elaine Wood
Inside Illustrations: Janet Armbrust
Cover Design: Matthew Van Zomeren
Photo Credits: Corel Corporation

McGraw-Hill
Children's Publishing
A Division of The McGraw-Hill Companies

Published by Instructional Fair • TS Denison
An imprint of McGraw-Hill Children's Publishing
Copyright © 1998 McGraw-Hill Children's Publishing

Send all inquiries to:
McGraw-Hill Children's Publishing
3195 Wilson Drive NW
Grand Rapids, Michigan 49544

Science Up to Standards—grades 5–8
ISBN: 1-56822-748-5

Table of Contents

To the Teacher

The science literacy of our citizens may well determine the path America chooses to follow in the future. In this day of rapidly expanding science technology, diminishing air and water quality, and dwindling natural resources, all adults must participate in science-based decisions. A successful America needs science-literate citizens.

In 1996 NSTA, the National Science Teachers' Association, released its plans to help schools improve science literacy. These plans, the National Science Education Standards, are designed as goals for every science program. The plans are called "standards" because they serve as criteria to judge all aspects of science education: quality of student knowledge, quality of science programs, quality of science teaching, quality of system support for teachers, quality of assessment practices, and progress toward the national vision of science literacy.

The National Science Education Standards include lists of science concepts that students should be taught. In addressing concepts appropriate for middle schoolers, the writers point out that even though middle school students are concrete thinkers, they are capable of comprehending some abstract science concepts. For example, they can understand that there should be a relationship between evidence and explanation. Similarly, they can understand that background knowledge and accepted theories help determine the design of current experiments and the interpretation of their data.

Students in this age group have some trouble designing their own scientific investigations. For one thing, it is difficult for them to identify variables and controls in an experiment. For another, they tend to interpret data in a way that agrees with their preconceived ideas. However, these problems are simply due to the level of maturity of the students and can be solved with teacher assistance.

For students in grades 5-8, the standards recommend an understanding of the process of scientific inquiry. Specifically, the standards suggest that teachers provide students with opportunities to perform full and partial inquiries. The standards support a generalized use of the "scientific method." They suggest that use of some or all of the steps of scientific inquiry can help students gain knowledge, engage in high-level reasoning, apply existing knowledge to science, and share scientific information with others.

In partial inquiries, some of the investigation is already planned and outlined for students, and they are asked to complete it. For example, the question to be tested may be stated and an investigation planned. Students then conduct the investigation, gather and analyze the data, and report their findings. In full inquiries, students recognize a question that can be answered through scientific inquiry. From that question, they conduct research, design an investigation, collect evidence, evaluate and interpret that evidence, and report it to others.

Teachers who prefer to omit the partial inquiry exercises and use only the full inquiry investigations may need to review students on the objective being met or on science techniques such as experimental design, data collection, and graphing. Remind students to test only one variable and to establish a control.

On the student activity pages of the full inquiry investigations, space is provided for five procedural steps. If more space is needed, students can write on their own paper. The Post-Lab Questions at the end of each full inquiry help students explain their conclusions.

Using This Resource Book to Meet the Standards

Science Up to Standards provides teachers with activities that cover the seven content areas recommended by the middle school science standards. These content areas are:
1. Scientific Inquiry
2. Physical Science
3. Life Science
4. Earth and Space Science
5. Science and Technology
6. Science in Personal and Social Perspectives
7. History and Nature of Science

Arranged in pairs of partial and full inquiry activities, *Science Up to Standards* is organized in a teacher-friendly fashion. Each pair of activities is prefaced by:
• a Teacher Information page that includes suggestions for introductory activities and grading rubrics for both activities. This page also specifies which NSTA objective is being addressed. From this NSTA objective, a very specific lab objective is derived.
• a Background Information page that provides students with enough knowledge to participate in both activities.

Two types of student activities follow the Teacher Information page and the Background Information page—a partial inquiry and a full inquiry.
The partial inquiry is presented first. In this exercise, a question or problem is stated, background information is provided, and an investigation is planned. Students complete the investigation and draw conclusions. Their conclusions lead them to interpret their results and present them to others. The partial inquiry teaches students an experimental technique, and provides them a model to follow in their own full inquiry.

In the full inquiry, students are presented with a question or problem. From this, they design an investigation which they can conduct to answer that question. Students gather their results, analyze them to draw conclusions, and present their findings to others. The skills or techniques needed to design and complete such an activity come from their own background knowledge and from the partial inquiry presented immediately before this full inquiry.

To facilitate the full inquiry technique, teachers are encouraged to avoid suggesting materials and procedures to students. A cart or box containing a variety of science supplies should be kept available for full inquiry investigations. This cart or box should include all of the materials students will actually need for their full inquiries plus some items that they will not need. Over time, students will learn to be efficient in their work and use only those lab supplies that they need.

SCIENCE AS INQUIRY

Identify questions that can be answered through scientific inquiry.

Design and conduct a scientific investigation.

Use appropriate tools and techniques to gather, analyze, and interpret data.

Develop descriptions, explanations, predictions, and models using evidence.

Think critically and logically to make the relationships between evidence and explanations.

Recognize and analyze alternative explanations and predictions.

Communicate scientific procedures and explanations.

Use mathematics in all aspects of scientific inquiry.

Understandings about scientific inquiry:

• Different kinds of questions suggest different kinds of scientific investigations. Some investigations involve observing and describing objects, organisms, or events; some involve collecting specimens; some involve experiments; some involve seeking more information; some involve discovery of new objects and phenomena; and some involve making models.

• Current scientific knowledge and understanding guide scientific investigations. Different scientific domains employ different methods, core theories, and standards to advance scientific knowledge and understanding.

• Mathematics is important in all aspects of scientific inquiry.

• Technology used to gather data enhances accuracy and allows scientists to analyze and quantify results of investigations.

- Scientific explanations emphasize evidence, have logically consistent arguments, and use scientific principles, models, and theories. The scientific community accepts and uses such explanations until displaced by better scientific ones. When such displacement occurs, science advances.

- Science advances through legitimate skepticism. Asking questions and querying other scientists' explanations is part of scientific inquiry. Scientists evaluate the explanations proposed by other scientists by examining evidence, comparing evidence, identifying faulty reasoning, pointing out statements that go beyond the evidence, and suggesting alternative explanations for the same observations.

- Scientific investigations sometimes result in new ideas and phenomena for study, generate new methods or procedures for an investigation, or develop new technologies to improve the collection of data. All of these results can lead to new investigations.

Dense Food & Are You Dense?

Teacher Information

NSTA
Objectives: A substance has characteristic properties, such as density, boiling point, and solubility, all of which are independent of the amount of the sample.

Specific
Objectives: Students will determine the densities of several materials.
Students will compare the densities of pre-1982 and post-1983 pennies.
Students will determine how a change in volume affects the density of marshmallows.

Time
Required for *Dense Food:* 50 minutes

Time
Required for *Are You Dense?:* This will vary with each student's proposed inquiry, but will require about two hours.

Teaching
Strategies: Copy the Background Information for Dense Food and Are You Dense? and the student activity pages of Dense Food for students. Marshmallows were chosen for Dense Food because they are easily compressed. Other compressible materials also work well.

To introduce the concept of density, have students compare the density of a small Tootsie Roll candy to the density of water. Water has a density of 1 g/ml (1 g/cm³). If something has a density greater than 1g/ml, it will sink in water. A substance whose density is less than the density of water will float in water. After students predict whether a Tootsie Roll is more or less dense than water, let them place one of the unwrapped candies in water to see if their predictions were correct.

In the partial inquiry lab, Dense Food, you may need to review the formula for determining the volume of a cylinder: $V = \pi r^2 h$ $(\pi = 3.14)$

With this formula, students can calculate the density of the Tootsie Roll and other cylindrical objects. The mass, length, radius, and volume of bite-sized Tootsie Rolls vary. Table 1 shows the average of actual measurements.

Table 1. Measurement of Bite-Sized Tootsie Rolls

Tootsie Roll mass	Varies, but average is 7 grams.
Tootsie Roll length	Varies, but average is 3 cm.
Tootsie Roll radius	Varies, but average is .5 cm.
Tootsie Roll volume	Varies, but average is 1.5 ml.
Tootsie Roll density	Varies, but average is 4 g/ml.

In the full inquiry Are You Dense? students will need copper wire, copper shot, or some other form of copper. If you use wire, choose a thick gauge so that it will displace a significant amount of water. Cut it into lengths that are several inches long, then coil or roll the wire so that it will fit into a graduated cylinder.

Provide pennies that were minted before 1982 and after 1983. Pennies minted before 1982 are 95% copper and 5% zinc. To save money, the U.S. mint started making pennies out of zinc and coating them with copper in 1983. During 1982 and 1983, several experimental formulas of pennies were minted. Pennies from those two years have variable compositions. The density of copper is 8.92 g/ml. The density of zinc is 7.14 g/ml.

In this experiment, students are asked to devise their own experiment to determine the density of several objects: a piece of copper wire, pre-1982 pennies, and post-1983 pennies. The appropriate way to determine the volumes of the wire and pennies is by water displacement. A penny has a volume of .36 ml. This is a difficult volume to read on a graduated cylinder. Encourage students to determine the volume of 25 pennies, then divide that volume by 25 to get the volume of one penny. A penny minted before 1982 weighs 3.1 g and one minted after 1983 weigh 2.5 g. (Pennies minted in 1982 were not the same composition as those minted in 1981 and 1983. They weigh 2.86 g, have a volume of .36 ml, and a density of 7.9 g/ml. If you use these pennies in the lab, the results will be confusing.)

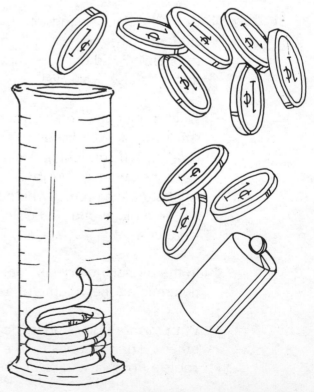

Dense Food

Are You Dense?

Think about the way you would describe water to an alien. You might say, "It's a colorless, odorless liquid that changes to steam at 100° C and freezes at 0° C." In this description, you have listed some physical properties of water. Whether you have a drop of water or a glass of water, you will find that the physical properties of water remain the same.

Substances, such as water, have some physical properties that are constant. These properties can be used to describe those substances. Color, boiling point, melting point, texture, and density are some of the physical properties of substances.

The density of a substance is related to its volume and mass. Volume refers to how much space the substance occupies. The mass of a substance is due to the amount of matter present in that substance. The density of a substance can be determined by dividing that substance's mass by its volume. The formula for density is:

$$D = M/V$$
Density = Mass/Volume

Think about the size and mass of a Ping-Pong ball and a golf ball. Although both occupy about the same amount of space, they have very different masses. Therefore, their densities are different. Can you explain why a Ping-Pong ball floats and a golf ball sinks? Which is more dense?

To calculate the density of an object, find its mass and volume. It is easy to find the mass of something; simply place it on a balance or scale. Volume can be calculated in one of four ways:

1. For objects with regular lengths, widths, and heights, multiply the three sides. For example, to determine the density of a block of wood, measure its three dimensions and multiply the measurements.

       Volume = Length x Width x Height
       Volume = 5 cm x 10 cm x 2 cm
       Volume = 100 cm³

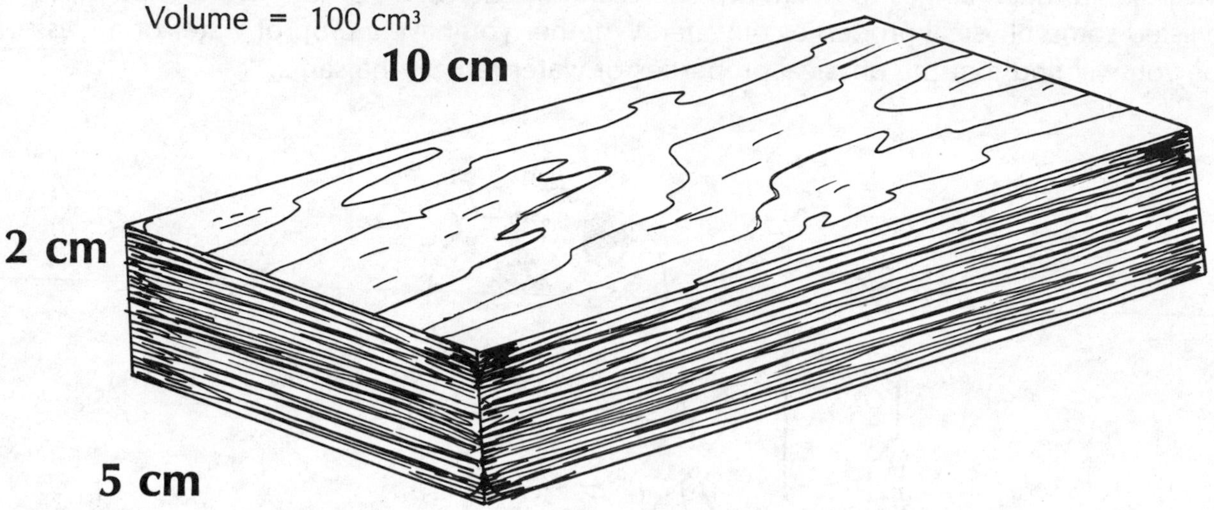

10 cm

2 cm

5 cm

Figure 1. Volume of a block can be determined by measurement.

2. Determine the volume of a liquid by pouring it into a graduated cylinder and reading the volume from the side of the cylinder.

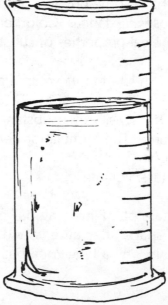

Figure 2. The volume of liquids can be found by pouring those liquids in a graduated cylinder.

3. If the object is irregularly shaped, use a method called *water displacement*. Small objects can be placed in a graduated cylinder that is partially filled with water. The new volume minus the original volume equals the volume of the sample.

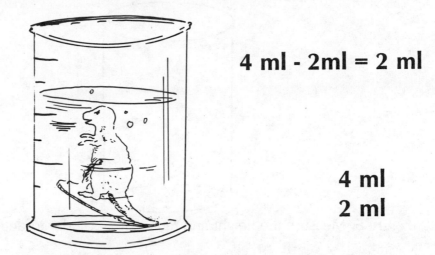

$$4 \text{ ml} - 2\text{ml} = 2 \text{ ml}$$

4 ml
2 ml

Figure 3. In water displacement, a little water is poured into a graduated cylinder. The volume is read, then the object whose volume is unknown is added to the water (Figure 3). Addition of the object causes the water level to rise. The difference between the first water level and the second water level equals the volume of the object.

If the sample is too large to fit in a graduated cylinder, place it in a water-filled container and place that container into a larger container. Measure the water that overflows into the larger container when the sample is added.

Figure 4. Place large, irregularly shaped samples in a container of water and place it inside another container (Figure 4). Fill the small container to the brim, then add the irregularly shaped sample. The water that is displaced out of the small container equals the volume of the irregularly shaped object. Measure displaced water by pouring it into a graduated cylinder.

4. To determine the volume of a cylinder, use the formula:

$$V = \pi r^2 h$$

Volume = π x radius squared x height

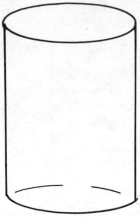

Figure 5. Measure the height and radius of a cylinder to determine its volume.

Pre-Lab Questions

1. What is *density*?

   _____

   _____

2. How can you determine the volume of an unknown amount of liquid found in a paper cup?

   _____

   _____

3. How could you use the volume that you determined in question #2 to find the density of that unknown liquid?

   _____

   _____

4. What is the volume of a box that is 1 foot tall, 3 feet long, and 2 feet wide?

   _____

   _____

5. You have 10 ml of water in a graduated cylinder. You add a small rock, and the volume of the water plus the rock is 16.6 ml. What is the volume of the rock?

   _____

   _____

6. Name some examples of physical properties.

   _____

   _____

7. The volume of a ripe tomato is 25 ml. The mass of that tomato is 50 grams. What is the density of the tomato?

   _____

   _____

Dense Food

A Partial Inquiry on Determining Density of Materials

Purpose: Determine the densities of several materials.
Determine how a change in volume affects the density of marshmallows.

Materials Needed: 500-ml beaker
50 miniature or 7 large marshmallows
Balance
Ruler

Procedure: 1. Use the balance to find the mass of a 500-ml beaker. Record this mass in the Data Table in row A.

2. Place 50 miniature or 7 large marshmallows in a beaker. Shake the beaker gently to evenly distribute the marshmallows (see Figure 1).

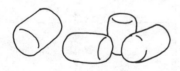 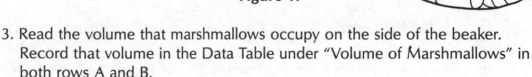

Figure 1.

3. Read the volume that marshmallows occupy on the side of the beaker. Record that volume in the Data Table under "Volume of Marshmallows" in both rows A and B.

4. Use the balance to find the mass of the beaker and marshmallows. Record this mass in the Data Table in row A.

5. To find the mass of the marshmallows, subtract the mass of the beaker from the total mass of the marshmallows plus the beaker. Record the mass of the marshmallows in the Data Table in row A.

6. Using the volume and mass of marshmallows, determine their density using the formula:

Density = Mass/Volume

Record density in row A.

7. With your hand, press the marshmallows down into the bottom of the beaker.

8. Read the volume of the compressed marshmallows and record that volume in the Data Table in row B.

9. Use the balance to find the mass of the compressed marshmallows and beaker. Record the mass in the Data Table in row B.

10. To find the mass of the compressed marshmallows, subtract the mass of the beaker from the mass of the marshmallows plus beaker. Record the mass of the compressed marshmallows in the Data Table in row B.

11. Using the volume and mass of the compressed marshmallows, determine their density and record in Row B. Use the formula that you used in Procedure step #6.

Data Table. Measurements of Beaker and Marshmallows in Beaker

Marshmallows	Mass of Beaker	Volume of Marshmallows	Mass of Beaker + Marshmallows	Mass of Marshmallows	Density of Marshmallows
A. Loosely Packed Marshmallows					
B. Tightly Packed Marshmallows					

Post-Lab Questions

1. Which marshmallows were the most dense, the loosely packed marshmallows or the compressed marshmallows?

_____

2. What two physical characteristics of marshmallows determine their density?

_____

3. What is one way of increasing the density of a material?

_____

4. How would you determine the volume of a marble?

_____

5. Write a short plan for determining the density of milk.

_____

Are You Dense?

A Full Inquiry on Determining the Density of Materials

Purpose: Determine the density of copper.

Compare the densities of pre-1982 and post-1983 pennies.

Materials Needed: _____

_____

_____

_____

Procedure: Design an experiment in which you can:

    a) determine the density of copper

    b) compare the densities of pre 1982-pennies and post-1983 pennies

Steps in Your Procedure

1. _____

_____

2. _____

_____

3. _____

_____

4. _____

_____

5. _____

_____

Results: Create your own data table if you need one.

_____

_____

_____

Your Data Table

Post-Lab Questions

1. What is the problem that you are trying to solve in this investigation?

   _____

   _____

2. How did you determine the density of copper?

   _____

   _____

3. How did you determine the densities of pre-1982 and post-1983 pennies?

   _____

   _____

4. From your results, can you conclude that all pennies are made of copper? Why or why not?

   _____

   _____

5. Did all of your pennies have the same density? If they did not, offer an explanation.

   _____

   _____

6. Copper is a very expensive metal. The cost of copper required to make one pure copper penny is more than one cent. How could the government save money on the manufacture of pennies?

   _____

   _____

Feed the Seed & Potash, Anyone?

Teacher Information

NSTA
Objectives: Mathematics is important in all aspects of scientific inquiry.
Scientific explanations emphasize evidence, have logically consistent arguments, and use scientific principles, models, and theories. The scientific community accepts and uses such explanations until displaced by better scientific ones. When such displacement occurs, science advances.

Specific
Objectives: Students gather evidence on the response of plants to varying amounts of nitrogen and potassium.

Time
Required for *Feed the Seed:* Day 1—30 minutes
Days 2 to 13—10 minutes
Day 14—1 hour

Time
Required for *Potash, Anyone?* Variable, to be determined by students. A reasonable length of time is 5 to 14 days. You may want to set some time limitations.

Teaching
Strategies: Copy Background Information and student activity pages for students. Have them read the Background Information on Feed the Seed and Potash, Anyone? and answer the questions.

As an introductory activity, show students some healthy, dark green plants and some pale, nutrient-deficient ones. Ask them to discuss some factors that might have caused the differences in these plants.

For the partial inquiry, Feed the Seed, prepare five solutions:
5% nitrogen water (5 g nitrogen fertilizer in a little water; stir, then add water to make a volume of 100 ml)
10% nitrogen water (10 g nitrogen fertilizer in a little water; stir, then add water to make a volume of 100 ml)
20% nitrogen water (20 g nitrogen fertilizer in a little water; stir, then add water to make a volume of 100 ml)

30% nitrogen water (30 g nitrogen fertilizer in a little water; stir, then add water to make a volume of 100 ml)

40% nitrogen water (40 g nitrogen fertilizer in a little water; stir, then add water to make a volume of 100 ml)

Nitrogen fertilizer can be purchased under the name ammonium nitrate.

In the full inquiry Potash, Anyone?, students will need fertilizer that contains potassium, such as potassium chloride (muriate of potash) which is 50% potassium or potassium sulfate (sulfate of potash) which is 38% potassium.

Either prepare potassium solutions for students, or instruct them to prepare their own.

Evaluation Rubrics

Name _____

Grading Rubric for Feed the Seed

Criteria	Points Possible	Points Awarded
Completed Data Table	25	_____
Drew graph to show growth of plants under varying conditions of nitrogen	25	_____
Pre-Lab Questions correct	25	_____
Post-Lab Questions correct	25	_____
Total	100	_____

Name _____

Grading Rubric for Potash, Anyone?

Criteria	Points Possible	Points Awarded
Listed materials	25	_____
Outlined a procedure	25	_____
Reported results	25	_____
Post-Lab Questions correct	25	_____
Total	100	_____

Feed the Seed
Potash, Anyone?

The condition of the soil is one of the most important factors in raising plants. Plants need nutrients or food, water, and minerals, just as you do. Without these nutrients, plants develop deficiency diseases. Two symptoms of nutrient deficiencies in plants are yellow leaves and leaves that fall off the plant.

When nutrients are not available in the soil, plants cannot grow correctly. Nutrients can be added to the soil by applying fertilizer. The amount and type of fertilizer added to plants is very important. Too much fertilizer causes plants to lose their fluids and die. If too little fertilizer is used, the plants lose leaves and turn yellow.

Most fertilizers contain three nutrients: nitrogen, phosphorus, and potassium (also called *potash*). The amounts of these three nutrients are represented by the formula found on the outside of fertilizer bags. If a fertilizer bag reads 10-20-20, the fertilizer inside is 10% nitrogen, 20% phosphorus, and 20% potassium. Other types of fertilizers may contain only one or two of these nutrients.

Nitrogen is a plant nutrient that helps plants maintain their dark green color. Nitrogen is also required for plant growth. Excess nitrogen causes rapid growth and weakness in the plant. However, some plants, such as lettuce, cabbage, and lawn grass, require extra nitrogen.

This bag contains 20% nitrogen, 10% phosphorus, and 10% potassium.

Phosphorus aids in production of flowers, seeds, and grains. It promotes good seed germination and healthy seedlings. Soil rich in phosphorus produces plants with colorful flowers and plump seeds.

Potassium (or potash) helps to control water movement into and out of the cells during food production. Plants that are potassium deficient have leaves that look scorched. They also have poor root systems. It is very unusual for plants to receive too much potassium. In the lab, you will investigate the effects of various levels of nutrients on plants. In one experiment, you will follow a plan that has already been written. In the other experiment, you will write your own plan.

When designing experimental plans, scientists follow a few logical steps. These steps are often called the *scientific method*. The steps include:

    a. State the problem. Before scientists can determine how their experiment will be designed, they clearly and precisely define the problem they are trying to solve.

    b. Research the problem. Some problems have already been solved, or at least partially solved by other experimenters. Find out what other people know about your problem.

    c. Based on your research, form a *hypothesis,* or a guess, about the answer to this problem.

    d. Design an experiment to test your hypothesis. Be certain that this experiment has only one variable. A *variable* is the factor in an experiment that is changed. You also need a *control,* or a part of the experiment where nothing is changed, to use as a comparison.

    e. Collect data. As you conduct your experiment, write down your findings. Sometimes it is helpful to record findings in a data table.

    f. Draw conclusions. Look at the data you collected and determine whether or not it answers your original question.

    g. Report findings. Let others know what you found out in your experiment. Findings can be shared in a lab report, a paper, an oral report, a poster, and in many other ways.

Pre-Lab Questions

1. Why do plants need nutrients?

    _____

    _____

2. Name three plant nutrients commonly found in fertilizers.

    _____

    _____

3. What are some signs of nutrient deficiency in plants?

    _____

    _____

4. What is the first step of the scientific method?

    _____

    _____

5. When using the scientific method, what should you do before you design an experiment? Why?

    _____

    _____

Name _____

Feed the Seed

Purpose: Using the scientific method, determine how various amounts of nitrogen affect the growth of radish seedlings.

Materials Needed:

Radish seeds	Ruler
Sand	Masking tape or labels
Six small paper cups	Graduated cylinder
Small shovel	Nitrogen fertilizer solutions (5% solution, 10%
Water	solution, 20% solution, 30% solution, and 40% solution

Procedure:

1. Label the cups as A, B, C, D, E, and F. With the tip of a pencil or ink pen, punch three or four holes in the bottom of each cup.

2. Add sand to all six cups so that the sand is 1 cm below the top of the cup (see Figure 1).

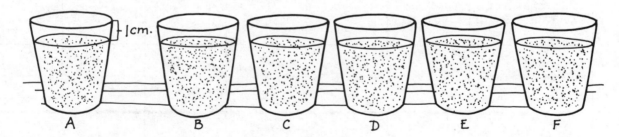

Figure 1. Add sand to within 1 cm of the top of each cup.

3. To each cup of sand, add five radish seeds. Stir the sand gently so that the radish seeds are barely covered.

4. Add water to each cup as follows:
   cup A with 30 ml of 5% nitrogen water,
   cup B with 30 ml of 10% nitrogen water,
   cup C with 30 ml of 20 % nitrogen water,
   cup D with 30 ml of 30% nitrogen water,
   cup E with 30 ml of 40% nitrogen water,
   cup F with 30 ml of tap water.

5. Place the cups in the sun, and water as needed with their appropriate water. When watering, give all cups the same amount.

6. When the seeds begin to germinate, enter the date of their germination in the Data Table. You will know that germination has begun when you see a leaf or root emerge from the seed.

7. Measure the young radish plants each day for two weeks. (To find the average length of radish plants in each cup, measure all five radish plants, add their lengths, then divide the total lengths by 5.) Also note the color of each seedling. Enter this information in the Data Table.

Data Table. Heights and Color of Each Radish Seedling

	Cup A	Cup B	Cup C	Cup D	Cup E	Cup F
Day 1: Average Length						
Color						
Day 2: Average Length						
Color						
Day 3: Average Length						
Color						
Day 4: Average Length						
Color						

Day 5: Average Length						
Color						
Day 6: Average Length						
Color						
Day 7: Average Length						
Color						
Day 8: Average Length						
Color						
Day 9: Average Length						
Color						
Day 10: Average Length						
Color						
Day 11: Average Length						
Color						

Day 12: Average Length						
Color						
Day 13: Average Length						
Color						
Day 14: Average Length						
Color						

Post-Lab Questions

1. What is the problem that you are trying to solve in this investigation?

_____

_____

2. What is the variable in this experiment?

_____

_____

3. What is the control in this experiment?

_____

_____

4. Which radish seeds grew to be the tallest?

_____

_____

5. Which radish seeds maintained a dark green color throughout the experiment?

_____

_____

6. On the graph below, depict the growth of seeds against the number of days, using the average length of all five plants each day. In your graph, use the following key, or graph each cup of radishes a different color:

- - - - - - - - = Cup A

******** = Cup B

-.-.-.-.- = Cup C

. . . . = Cup D

^^^^^^ = Cup E

++++++ = Cup F

Graph. Average Length of Radish Plants Each Day

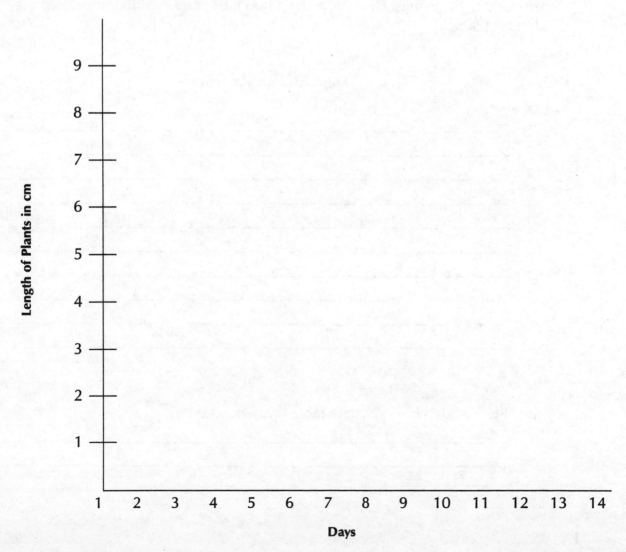

Potash, Anyone?

A Full Inquiry on Using the Scientific Method

Purpose: Using the scientific method, determine how varying amounts of potassium (also called *potash*) affect the growth of seedlings.

Materials Needed: _____
_____
_____
_____

Procedure: Design an experiment in which you vary the amount of potassium fed to developing seedlings. Determine the amount of potassium that produces the largest plants.

Steps in Your Procedure

1. _____
_____
2. _____
_____
3. _____
_____
4. _____
_____
5. _____
_____

Results: Create your own data table if you need one.

_____
_____
_____

Your Data Table

Post-Lab Questions

1. What is the problem that you are trying to solve in this investigation?

   _____

   _____

2. What was the variable in this investigation?

   _____

   _____

3. What was the control in this investigation?

   _____

   _____

4. What is the ideal amount of potassium to feed to seedlings? Why?

   _____

   _____

5. Describe the appearance of plants grown without any potassium.

   _____

   _____

6. Describe the appearance of plants grown with an excessive amount of potassium.

   _____

   _____

7. Plants need a variety of nutrients. Were these experimental radishes receiving any nutrients besides potassium?

   _____

   _____

PHYSICAL SCIENCE

Properties and Changes of Properties in Matter
• A substance has characteristic properties, such as density, boiling point, and solubility, all of which are independent of the amount of the samples. A mixture of substances often can be separated into the original substances using one or more of the characteristic properties.

• Substances react chemically in characteristic ways with other substances to form new substances (compounds) with different characteristic properties. In chemical reactions, the total mass is conserved. Substances often are placed in categories or groups if they react in similar ways; metals are an example of such a group.

• Chemical elements do not break down during normal laboratory reactions involving such treatments as heating, exposure to electric current, or reaction with acids. There are more than 100 known elements that combine in a multitude of ways to produce compounds, which account for the living and nonliving substances that we encounter.

Motions and Forces
• The motion of an object can be described by its position, direction, and speed. That motion can be measured and represented on a graph.

• An object that is not being subjected to a force will continue to move at a constant speed and in a straight line.

• If more than one force acts on an object along a straight line, then the forces will reinforce or cancel one another, depending on their direction and magnitude. Unbalanced forces will cause changes in the speed or direction of an object's motion.

Transfer of Energy
• Energy is a property of many substances and is associated with heat, light, electricity, mechanical motion, sound, nuclei, and the nature of a chemical. Energy is transferred in many ways.

• Heat moves in predictable ways, flowing from warmer objects to cooler ones, until both reach the same temperature.

- Light interacts with matter by transmission (including refraction), absorption, or scattering (including reflection). To see an object, light from that object—emitted by or scattered from it—must enter the eye.

- Electrical circuits provide a means of transferring electrical energy when heat, light, sound, and chemical changes are produced.

- In most chemical and nuclear reactions, energy is transferred into or out of a system. Heat, light, mechanical motion, or electricity might all be involved in such transfers.

- The sun is a major source of energy for changes on the earth's surface. The sun loses energy by emitting light. A tiny fraction of that light reaches the earth, transferring energy from the sun to the earth. The sun's energy arrives as light with a range of wavelengths, consisting of visible light, infrared, and ultraviolet radiation.

The Force Is with Us & Speed On!

Teacher Information

NSTA
Objectives: The motion of an object can be described by its position, direction, and speed. That motion can be measured and represented on a graph.

Specific
Objectives: Determine the effect that changes in mass and speed of a force have on the inertia of an object at rest.

Time
Required for *The Force Is with Us:* 50 minutes

Time
Required for *Speed On!* Times will vary according to the investigation chosen by students. One class period should be sufficient for most students. You may want to establish time limits for this activity.

Teaching
Strategies: Copy the Background Information and the student activity pages for The Force Is with Us and Speed On! Have students read this information and complete the Pre-Lab Questions.

As an introductory activity, discuss *inertia* with your students. For example, review what occurs when a parked car is struck by an oncoming truck. The force of the truck against the parked car causes the car to move forward. The forward movement occurs because the force of the truck overcomes the inertia of the parked car. Remind students that this is an example of Newton's First Law of Motion.

For this lab, you will need some metal weights of various sizes and some strong twine to make a pendulum. A small cardboard box can serve as the object to be moved.

Evaluation Rubrics

Name _____

Grading Rubric for The Force Is with Us

Criteria	Points Possible	Points Awarded
Pre-Lab Questions correct	35	_____
Data Table correct	30	_____
Post-Lab Questions correct	35	_____
Total	100	_____

Name _____

Grading Rubric for Speed On!

Criteria	Points Possible	Points Awarded
Outline of plan for experiment	25	_____
Carried out procedure according to plan	50	_____
Post-Lab Questions correct	25	_____
Total	100	_____

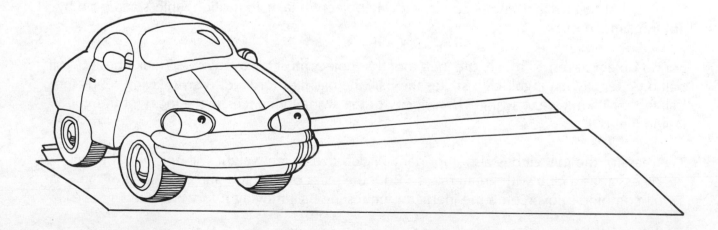

The Force Is with Us & Speed On!

In the seventeenth century, Sir Isaac Newton studied the relationships between force and motion. Through his studies, he developed what we now call Newton's Three Laws of Motion.

Newton's first law of motion is based on changes in an object's inertia due to unbalanced forces. *Unbalanced forces* are those that are not canceled by equal and opposite forces. For example, when you push a child in a swing, you exert an unbalanced force against the child and swing. This force causes the swing to move forward (see Figure 1).

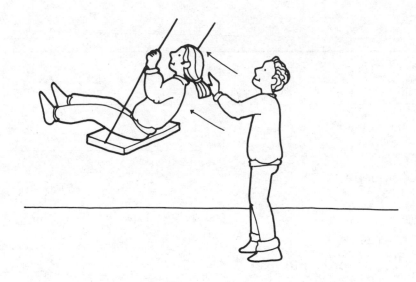

Figure 1.

Inertia is an object's resistance to change of position. Objects at rest do not have unbalanced forces acting on them. *Newton's first law of motion* (also called the law of inertia) states that an object at rest remains at rest, and a moving object remains in motion, unless acted on by an unbalanced force.

For an object at rest to move, the inertia of that object must be overcome. Think about a golf ball on a tee. When a golf club strikes the ball, the ball flies forward. A swift swing sends the ball farther than a weak swing. The velocity of the swing influences the velocity of the golf ball in flight.

The mass of the golf club is also important. A club that is lightweight will not send the ball nearly as far as a club with greater mass. Both the mass of the club and the speed of the swing combine to overcome the inertia of the resting ball, moving it forward (see Figure 2).

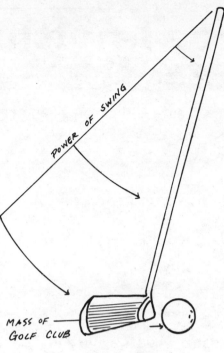

Figure 2.

Pre-Lab Questions:

1. State Newton's first law of motion.

_____

_____

2. Define *inertia*.

_____

_____

3. Explain the effect that unbalanced forces have on the inertia of a stationary object.

_____

_____

4. Explain why Newton's first law of motion describes how a seat belt prevents a passenger in a car wreck from going through the windshield.

_____

_____

5. How does Newton's first law of motion explain the fact that a bowling ball can knock down bowling pins?

_____

_____

The Force Is with Us

A Partial Inquiry on Newton's First Law of Motion

Purpose: Determine the effect that a change in the mass of a force has on the inertia of an object at rest.

Materials Needed: A small cardboard box (such as a small jewelry box)
A piece of twine
Several metal weights (suggested sizes are 50 g, 100 g, and 200 g)
A metric ruler
The edge of a table or desk
Masking tape or duct tape

Procedure: 1. Cut a piece of twine so that when it is taped to the edge of a table, the free end of the twine touches the floor (see Figure 3).

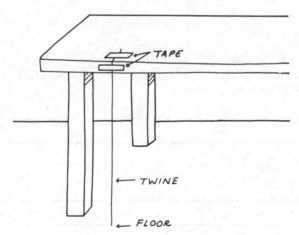

Figure 3. Cut the twine so the free end barely touching the floor.

2. Securely tape one end of the twine to the table.

3. Tie the free end of the twine to a 50-gram weight so that the string and weight can swing back and forth freely, without touching the floor. You have created a pendulum with your string and weight.

4. Allow the weight to hang straight down. Place a small box directly in front of the weight. You should have your pendulum and box arranged so that when set in motion, the swinging weight strikes the box and moves it forward.

5. Mark the original location of the box on the floor with a small piece of masking tape.

6. Pull the weight back so that it is 12 cm from the floor (see Figure 4). From this point, release the weight to swing toward the box.

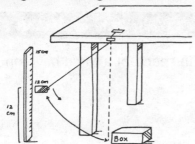

Mass	Trial 1	Trial 2	Trial 3	Average
50 g				
100 g				
200 g				

Figure 4. Pull back the weight so it is 12 cm above the floor.

7. Create a Data Table like the one above on a separate sheet of paper.

8. After the weight strikes the box, measure the distance the box moves from its original location. Record this distance in centimeters in your Data Table beside Trial 1 in 50-gram mass column.

9. Reset the box and perform steps 6 and 7 two more times. Record these distances in the Data Table beside Trial 2 and Trial 3. Calculate the average of the three trials by dividing the sum of these distances by three. Enter the average in your Data Table.

10. Perform the above steps again, but change the 50-gram weight to 100 grams. Be certain to pull the weight back to a height of 12 cm and use the same box. Measure the distance the box moves during three trials and record your average in your Data Table.

11. Repeat the above procedure, change the 100-gram weight for the 200-gram weight. Use the same box. Pull the weight back 12 cm, and record the distance the box moves from its original position. Do this three times. Calculate the average of the three distances.

Post-Lab Questions

1. What is the problem you are trying to solve in this activity?

2. Each time the mass of the swinging weight is increased, the box moves farther. What does this tell you about mass, force, and distance?

3. In this lab which object is originally "at rest"?

4. What happens to a standing passenger on a bus when the bus accelerates suddenly? Why?

Speed On!

A Full Inquiry on Newton's First Law of Motion

Purpose: Determine the effect that changes in speed of a force have on the inertia of an object at rest.

Materials Needed: _____

_____

_____

_____

Procedure: Design an experiment in which you measure the effect a change in the speed of a force has on the inertia of a resting object.

Steps in Your Procedure

1. _____

_____

2. _____

_____

3. _____

_____

4. _____

_____

5. _____

_____

Results: Create your own data table if you need one.

Your Data Table

Post-Lab Questions

1. What is the problem that you are trying to solve in this investigation?

_____

_____

_____

2. In this activity, how did you simulate forces with different speeds?

_____

_____

_____

3. What effect did increasing the speed of an object have on the inertia of a resting object?

_____

_____

_____

4. In which case will a parked car be moved farther: if hit by a truck moving at 5 miles per hour, or a truck moving at 55 miles per hour? Why?

_____

_____

_____

What's Your Reaction? & Ocean Winds

Teacher Information

NSTA
Objectives: Substances react chemically in characteristic ways with other substances to form new substances (compounds) with different characteristic properties. In chemical reactions, the total mass is conserved. Substances often are placed in categories or groups if they react in similar ways; metals are an example of such a group.

Specific
Objectives: Students will differentiate the conditions that affect the rate of chemical changes in iron.

Students will determine the effects that sodium chloride, table salt, has on rusting.

Time
Required for *What's Your Reaction?*: Day 1—30 minutes
Day 2—10 minutes
Day 3—20 minutes

Time
Required for *Ocean Winds*: Times will vary according to the investigation chosen by students. Part of the class period during a two- to three-day time span will probably be adequate. You will probably want to place a time limit on the length of the investigation.

Teaching
Strategies: Copy the Background Information and the student activity pages for What's Your Reaction? and Ocean Winds. Have students read this information and complete the Pre-Lab Questions.

To prepare for the introductory activity, place a piece of steel wool in water two days prior to the lab. Add about 5 ml of hydrogen peroxide. Hydrogen peroxide breaks down into water and oxygen. On the day of the lab, show students a piece of new steel wool. Explain to them that steel wool is made of iron. Then show them the piece of steel wool that has been in water and hydrogen peroxide for two days. Indicate that a new compound, iron oxide (rust) is now present.

For this lab, you will need to purchase some steel wool at a grocery or hardware store. It also can be ordered from chemical supply companies. Avoid buying steel wool with soap. You will also need some calcium chloride and sodium chloride. Sodium chloride can be purchased as table salt. Calcium chloride can be ordered through a chemical supply company or purchased at a hardware store as a de-icer.

Remind students to wear their goggles when they are working with chemicals. Also caution them about touching hot glassware when they use the hot plates.

Evaluation Rubrics

Name _____

Grading Rubric for What's Your Reaction?

Criteria	Points Possible	Points Awarded
Pre-Lab Questions correct	35	_____
Data Table correct	30	_____
Post-Lab Questions correct	35	_____
Total	100	_____

Name _____

Grading Rubric for Ocean Winds

Criteria	Points Possible	Points Awarded
Outlined plan for procedure	25	_____
Carried out procedure according to plan	50	_____
Post-Lab Questions correct	25	_____
Total	100	_____

What's Your Reaction?

Ocean Winds

All around you, chemical changes are occurring. Inside your body, for example, chemical changes are taking place. The oxygen you inhale is constantly combining with the nutrients from your food. This reaction creates energy that keeps you alive and allows you to perform your daily activities.

Materials can be changed in two ways: physically and chemically. In a physical change, the composition of the material is not affected. Freezing, cutting, melting, and crushing are examples of physical changes. These changes do not alter the properties of the original material. When ice melts, water freezes, or it vaporizes, you still have the original material, water. It has not changed to another material (Figure 1).

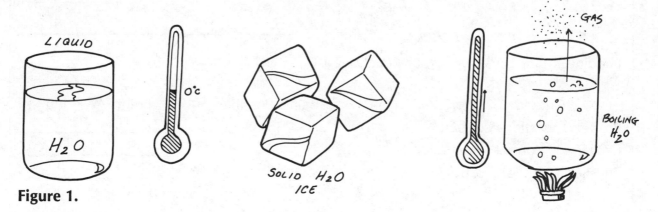

Figure 1.

In a chemical change, a new substance is formed that has different properties from the original material. When vinegar is combined with baking soda, bubbling and fizzing take place. Bubbles indicate that a gas has been formed. The gas produced in this chemical change is carbon dioxide. The gas has properties very different from the vinegar and baking soda. This is because the particles that make up vinegar and baking soda have been rearranged into particles of carbon dioxide (see Figure 2). This rearrangement creates a new substance with its own unique properties.

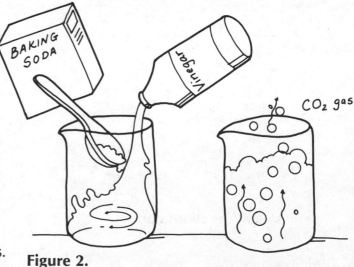

Figure 2.

The combination of oxygen with a material is also a chemical change because a new compound is formed. The new compound is called an *oxide*. For example, aluminum combines with oxygen in the air to produce aluminum oxide (see Figure 3). The formation of aluminum oxide from aluminum is another example of a chemical change.

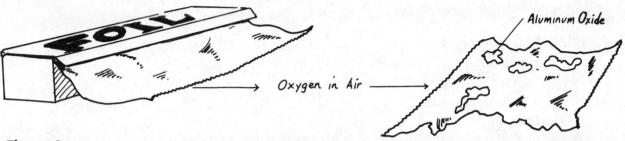

Figure 3.

Iron is another metal that forms an oxide. As iron combines with oxygen, it forms iron oxide or *rust*. Some metals, such as zinc, do not react with oxygen. Therefore, they are often used to coat iron and prevent it from combining with oxygen in the air.

Anyone who owns tools made of steel (iron) must be concerned with the chemical change called *rusting*. Leaving tools outdoors or in moist areas exposes the iron to oxygen. If these tools are not coated with a protective metal, they will readily form rust. The presence of moisture in the environment speeds rusting.

Pre-Lab Questions

1. Explain the difference between a chemical and a physical change.

   _____

   _____

2. How do you know that a chemical change occurs when you add vinegar to baking soda?

   _____

   _____

3. When water boils it forms a vapor. Is this a chemical or a physical change? Explain your answer.

   _____

   _____

4. What substance must be available for iron to rust?

   _____

   _____

5. How can you prevent an iron object from rusting?

   _____

   _____

What's Your Reaction?

A Partial Inquiry on Chemical Changes

Purpose: Differentiate the conditions that affect the rate of chemical changes in iron.

Materials Needed: Five test tubes
Five small pieces of steel wool (iron)
Water
Calcium chloride
Spatula
Hot plate
Hot pad
Beaker, 200-ml
Three test tube stoppers
Hydrogen peroxide
Graduated cylinder
Test tube rack
Grease pencil or masking tape and pen
Safety glasses

Procedure: 1. Place 50 ml of water in a beaker.

2. Place the beaker on a hot plate on a high temperature setting. Boil the water five minutes, then turn off the hot plate. Set this water aside to use in step 5.

3. Label the test tubes as A, B, C, D, and E (Figure 4).

4. Add a small piece of steel wool to each test tube.

5. Add the following to each test tube:
Test tube A—10 ml of tap water. Cover the test tube with a stopper.
Test tube B—10 ml of tap water and 5 ml of hydrogen peroxide.
Hydrogen peroxide breaks down into water and oxygen.
Cover with a stopper.
Test tube C—10 ml of boiled water. Boiling removes dissolved gases, such as oxygen and carbon dioxide, from water. Add a stopper.
Test tube D—10 ml of tap water and one-half teaspoon of calcium chloride. Calcium chloride absorbs oxygen. Do not add a stopper.
Test tube E—10 ml of tap water. Do not add a stopper.

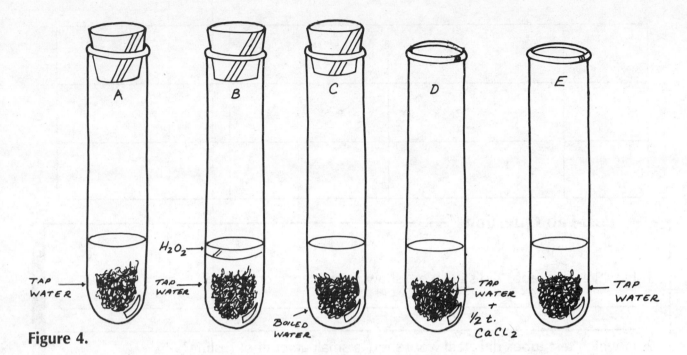

Figure 4.

6. In the Data Table, describe the appearance of each of the pieces of steel wool under the column "Appearance of iron at beginning of experiment."

7. Place the five test tubes in a test tube rack and set aside overnight.

8. The next day observe the steel wool in each test tube. In the Data Table, record changes in the steel wool under "Appearance of iron after 24 hours." Again, set the test tubes aside overnight.

9. The following day observe the test tubes. Indicate on the Data Table any changes that have occurred under the column "Appearance of iron after 48 hours."

Data Table. Changes in Steel Wool Observed in Two days

Test tube	Appearance of iron at beginning of experiment	Appearance of iron after 24 hours	Appearance of iron after 48 hours
A			
B			

C			
D			
E			

Post-Lab Questions

1. In which test tubes did steel wool show no evidence of rusting?

   _____

   _____

2. In which test tubes did steel wool show a small amount of rusting?

   _____

   _____

3. In which test tubes did steel wool show a great deal of rusting?

   _____

   _____

4. What substance is removed from water when water is boiled? Did your results support this? Explain.

   _____

   _____

5. What substance does calcium chloride remove from water? Did your results support this? Explain.

   _____

   _____

6. What substance does hydrogen peroxide add to water? Did your results support this? Explain.

   _____

   _____

7. Name the two substances that combine to form rust.

   _____

   _____

8. Why is formation of rust considered a chemical change?

   _____

   _____

Ocean Winds

A Full Inquiry on Chemical Changes

Purpose: Determine the effect sodium chloride (table salt) has on the rate of rusting.

Materials Needed: _____

_____

_____

_____

Procedure: Design an experiment in which you measure the effect salt water has on the rate at which iron rusts.

Steps in Your Procedure

1. _____

_____

2. _____

_____

3. _____

_____

4. _____

_____

5. _____

_____

Results: Create your own data table if you need one.

Your Data Table

Post-Lab Questions

1. What is the problem that you are trying to solve in this investigation?

   _____

   _____

2. What was the variable in this investigation?

   _____

   _____

3. What was the control in this investigation?

   _____

   _____

4. How does salt affect the rate at which iron rusts?

   _____

   _____

5. Use the information gathered from this lab to explain why iron structures located near the ocean seem to rust more quickly than similar structures a hundred miles from the ocean. Did the results of your lab support this observation?

   _____

   _____

3

LIFE SCIENCE

Structure and Function in Living Systems
• Living systems at all levels of organization demonstrate the complementary nature of structure and function. Important levels of organization for structure and function include cells, organs, tissues, organ systems, whole organisms, and ecosystems.

• All organisms are composed of cells—the fundamental units of life. Most organisms are single cells; other organisms, including humans, are multicellular.

• Cells carry on the many functions needed to sustain life. They grow and divide, thereby producing more cells. This requires that they take in nutrients, which they use to provide energy for the work that cells do or an organism needs.

• Specialized cells perform specialized functions in multicellular organisms. Groups of specialized cells cooperate to form a tissue, such as muscle. Different tissues are in turn grouped together to form larger functional units, called *organs*. Each type of cell, tissue, and organ has a distinct structure and set of functions that serve the organism as a whole.

• The human organism has systems for digestion, respiration, reproduction, circulation, excretion, movement, control, coordination, and for protection from disease. These systems interact with one another.

• Disease is a breakdown in structures or functions of an organism. Some diseases are the result of intrinsic failures of the system. Others are the result of damage by infection by other organisms.

Reproduction and Heredity
• Reproduction is a characteristic of all living systems. Because no individual organism lives forever, reproduction is essential to the continuation of every species. Some organisms reproduce sexually.

• In many species, including humans, females produce eggs and males produce sperm. Plants also reproduce sexually—the egg and sperm are produced in the flowers of flowering plants. An egg and sperm unite to begin development of a new individual. That new individual receives genetic information from its mother (via the egg) and its father (via the sperm). Sexually produced offspring never are identical to either of their parents.

- Every organism requires a set of instructions for specifying its traits. Heredity is the passage of these instructions from one generation to another.

- Hereditary information is contained in genes, located in the chromosomes of each cell. Each gene carries a single unit of information. An inherited trait of an individual can be determined by one or by many genes, and a single gene can influence more than one trait. A human cell contains many thousands of different genes.

- The characteristics of an organism can be described in terms of a combination of traits. Some traits are inherited and others result from interactions with the environment.

Regulation and Behavior
- All organisms must be able to obtain and use resources, grow, reproduce, and maintain stable internal conditions while living in a constantly changing external environment.

- Regulation of an organism's internal environment involves sensing the internal environment and changing physiological activities to keep conditions within the range required to survive.

- Behavior is one kind of response an organism can make to an internal or environmental stimulus. A behavioral response requires coordination and communication at many levels, including cells, organ systems, and whole organisms. Behavioral response is a set of actions determined in part by heredity and in part from experience.

- An organism's behavior evolves through adaptation to its environment. How a species moves, obtains food, reproduces, and responds to danger are based on the species' evolutionary history.

Populations and Ecosystems
- A population consists of all individuals of a species that are found together at a given place and time. All populations living together and the physical factors with which they interact compose an ecosystem.

- Populations of organisms can be categorized by the function they serve in an ecosystem. Plants and some microorganisms are producers—they make their own food. All animals, including humans, are consumers, which obtain food by eating other organisms. Decomposers, primarily bacteria and fungi, are consumers that use waste materials and dead organisms for food. Food webs identify the relationships among producers, consumers, and decomposers in an ecosystem.

- For ecosystems, the major source of energy is sunlight. Energy entering ecosystems as sunlight is transferred by producers into chemical energy through photosynthesis. That energy then passes from organism to organism in food webs.

- The number of organisms an ecosystem can support depends on the resources available and abiotic factors, such as quantity of light and water, range of temperatures, and soil composition. Given adequate biotic and abiotic resources and no disease or predators, populations (including humans) increase at rapid rates. Lack of resources and other factors, such as predation and climate, limit the growth of populations in specific niches in the ecosystem.

Diversity and Adaptations of Organisms
- Millions of species of animals, plants, and microorganisms are alive today. Although different species might look dissimilar, the unity among organisms becomes apparent from an analysis of internal structures, the similarity of their chemical processes, and the evidence of common ancestry.

- Biological evolution accounts for the diversity of species developed through gradual processes over many generations. Species acquire many of their unique characteristics through biological adaptation, which involves the selection of naturally occurring variation in populations. Biological adaptations include changes in structures, behaviors, or physiology that enhance survival and reproductive success in a particular environment.

- Extinction of a species occurs when the environment changes and the adaptive characteristics of a species are insufficient to allow its survival. Fossils indicate that many organisms that lived long ago are extinct. Extinction of species is common; most of the species that have lived on the earth no longer exist.

No UV on Me & Stay Cool

Teacher Information

NSTA
Objectives: Cells carry on the many functions needed to sustain life. They grow and divide, thereby producing more cells. This requires that they take in nutrients, which they use to provide energy for the work that cells do or an organism needs.

Regulation of an organism's internal environment involves sensing the internal environment and changing physiological activities to keep conditions within the range required to survive.

Specific
Objectives: Students will determine the effects of UV radiation and cold temperatures on the survival of yeast cells.

Time
Required for *No UV on Me*: Day 1—1 hour
Day 2 to 4—30 minutes
Day 5—1 hour

Time
Required for *Stay Cool*: Time will vary, depending on each student's investigation. Students will probably need a portion of two to five days. You may want to set some time limitations.

Teaching
Strategies: Copy the Background Information and the student activity pages. Have students read the Background Information on No UV on Me and Stay Cool and answer the Pre-Lab Questions.

As an introductory activity, let students view yeast cells under the microscope. The day before lab, mix a package of active, dry yeast with a tablespoon of sugar and a cup of warm water. On lab day, place a drop of the yeast mixture on a slide, add a cover slip, and view under the microscope. This exercise will ensure that students can identify yeast.

"Black" or UV (ultraviolet) lights are popular with young people because they make certain paints and dyes glow. However, UV radiation can damage the eyes. Students should not look directly at UV light. UV lights are available at pet stores, home decorator centers, some tape/CD stores, and many department stores.

Evaluation Rubrics

Name _____

Grading Rubric for No UV on Me

Criteria	Points Possible	Points Awarded
Data Table completed	25	_____
Drew graph to show population growth	25	_____
Pre-Lab Questions correct	25	_____
Post-Lab Questions correct	25	_____
Total	100	_____

Name _____

Grading Rubric for Stay Cool

Criteria	Points Possible	Points Awarded
Listed materials	25	_____
Outlined a procedure	25	_____
Reported results	25	_____
Post-Lab Questions correct	25	_____
Total	100	_____

No UV on Me

& Stay Cool

Have you ever eaten a mushroom pizza? Perhaps you have cleaned mildew from the shower floor. Mushrooms and mildews are two examples of fungi. *Fungi* are living things that are distinguished by the following characteristics:

a. They cannot make their own food. Fungi eat by spreading their digestive juices on their food, then soaking up the food.

b. Fungi cannot move from place to place. Like plants, these living things remain in one location.

c. Fungi have cell walls. All types of cells are surrounded by cell membranes. Fungi, plants, and some bacteria have stiff, protective cell walls around their cell membranes.

Most fungi are made of millions of cells. Yeast is one of the few one-celled fungi. Some types of yeast are commercially important because they can convert sugar to alcohol and carbon dioxide, a gas. These yeasts are used in the manufacture of bread, in which their carbon dioxide gas makes the bread rise. They are also important in the production of alcoholic beverages (Figure 1).

Yeast + sugar ——————> alcohol + carbon dioxide gas (CO_2).

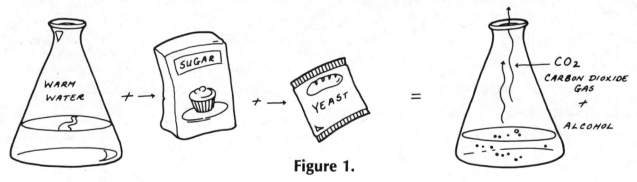

Figure 1.

A cell is the basic unit of life. Like all cells, yeast cells carry out all life processes. Each cell absorbs food and water, grows, and reproduces. To survive, a yeast cell must be in an environment where it can carry out its life processes. If the quality of its environment changes a small amount, a yeast cell can usually adjust and survive. However, drastic changes in the environment may cause a yeast cell to die. It may not be able to maintain the internal conditions required for life.

Some of the factors that affect the environment of living things are temperature, availability of water, light, and oxygen, and the presence of ultraviolet radiation. Most living things on earth are exposed to some UV radiation from the sun. This radiation travels to earth with the rest of the sun's energy (Figure 2). You are most aware of visible light energy from the sun. UV radiation generally goes unnoticed because it is invisible.

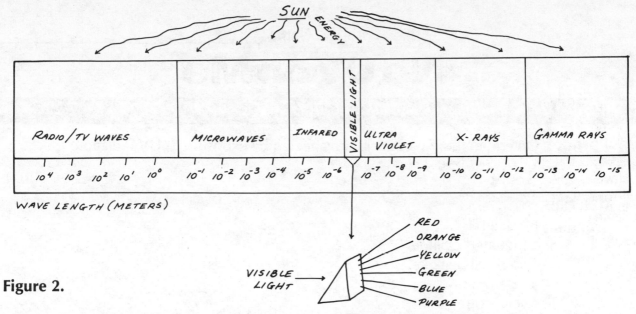

Figure 2.

Large amounts of UV radiation can be harmful to living things. Some people expose themselves to artificial UV radiation. Tanning beds and black lights are two man-made sources of UV radiation that may cause sunburn, skin cancer, and eye damage. Many living things do not tolerate large amounts of UV radiation.

Pre-Lab Questions

1. Describe the characteristics of fungi.

_____

_____

2. What is UV radiation? What is the source of most UV radiation?

_____

_____

3. Why is UV radiation dangerous?

_____

_____

4. What are two commercially important products that depend on the breakdown of sugar by yeast?

_____

_____

5. What is a cell? What are some functions of cells?

_____

_____

No UV on Me

A Partial Inquiry on Responses of Yeast Cells to High Levels of Exposure to UV Radiation

Purpose: Determine how yeast cells are affected by exposure to UV radiation.

Materials Needed:
Black light
Graduated cylinder
Two small beakers
Yeast-sugar-water mixture
Microscopes
Dropper
Slides
Cover slips
Grease pencil

Procedure: 1. Label two small beakers as A and B. Place 5 ml of yeast-sugar-water mixture in both beakers.

2. Remove a drop of yeast-sugar-water mixture from beaker A. Place this drop on a slide and cover the drop with a cover slip. View the drop using low power of the microscope.

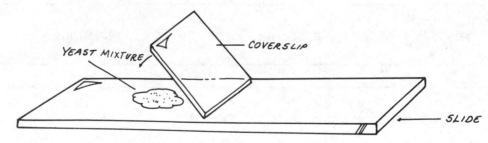

Figure 3.

3. Change the microscope to medium power and focus. Count the number of yeast cells you see. Enter the total number of cells in the Data Table in column A beside "Day 1: Number of yeast cells."

4. Rinse the slide. Repeat Procedure step #2 two more times. Enter all of your counts in column A beside "Day 1."

5. Add the number of yeast cells from all three counts, and divide the total by 3. Enter this average under A beside "Day 1."

6. Rinse the slide and repeat Procedure steps #2 through #5 for yeast in beaker B.

7. Place beaker A in a warm, dark place. Place beaker B under a UV light. Leave the beakers in these positions overnight.

Caution: UV light can damage your eyes. Do not look directly at the light.

8. Each day for the next four days, count the yeast cells in beakers A and B three times. Find the average of your counts. Enter this information in the Data Table.

Data Table. Average Number of Yeast Cells Each Day

	A	B
Day 1: Number of Yeast Cells	1. 2. 3. Ave.	1. 2. 3. Ave.
Day 2: Number of Yeast Cells	1. 2. 3. Ave.	1. 2. 3. Ave.
Day 3: Number of Yeast Cells	1. 2. 3. Ave.	1. 2. 3. Ave.
Day 4: Number of Yeast Cells	1. 2. 3. Ave.	1. 2. 3. Ave.
Day 5: Number of Yeast Cells	1. 2. 3. Ave.	1. 2. 3. Ave.

— Post-Lab Questions —

1. What is the problem that you are trying to solve, or the question that you are asking in this investigation?

   _____

   _____

2. What is the variable in this experiment?

   _____

   _____

3. What is the control in this experiment?

   _____

   _____

4. In which beaker did yeast cells grow best?

   _____

   _____

5. On the following graph, show the change in population of yeast cells, using the averages from each day. In your graph, use the following key, or indicate each group of yeast cells with a different color:

   - - - - - - = A   ******** = B

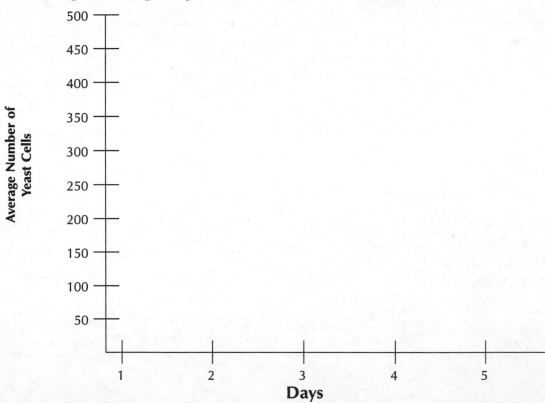

Graph. Average Population of Yeast Cells in Beakers A and B Each Day

Name _____

Stay Cool

Purpose: Determine how growth of yeast cells is affected by cold temperatures.

Materials Needed: _____

_____

_____

_____

Procedure: Design an experiment that demonstrates how the growth of yeast cells is affected by cold temperatures.

Steps of Your Procedure

1. _____

_____

2. _____

_____

3. _____

_____

4. _____

_____

5. _____

_____

Results: Create your own data table if you need one.

_____

_____

_____

Your Data Table

Post-Lab Questions

1. What is the problem you are trying to solve in this investigation?

   _____

   _____

2. What was the variable in this investigation?

   _____

   _____

3. What was the control in this investigation?

   _____

   _____

4. What conclusions can you draw from this investigation?

   _____

   _____

5. If you decided to grow as many yeast cells as possible, where would you grow them?

   _____

   _____

6. If you are using yeast to prepare bread, where should you put your bread dough while it is rising—in the refrigerator, in a hot oven, in a slightly warm oven? Why?

   _____

   _____

Hairy Kitty Cat Genes & Kitty Cat Toes

Teacher Information

NSTA Objectives: Most of the cells in a human can contain two copies of each of 22 different chromosomes. In addition, there is a pair of chromosomes that determines sex; a female contains two X chromosomes and a male contains one X and one Y chromosome. Transmission of genetic information to offspring occurs through egg and sperm cells that contains only one representative from each chromosome pair. An egg and a sperm unite to form a new individual. The fact that the human body is formed from cells that contain two copies of each chromosome—and therefore two copies of each gene—explains many features of human heredity, such as how variations that are hidden in one generation can be expressed in the next.

Specific Objectives: Students will determine the probable percentage of short-haired kittens that will be produced if a hybrid, short-haired female is bred with a long-haired male.

Students will determine the probable percentage of five-toed cats that will be produced if a pure six-toed female is bred with a hybrid six-toed male.

Time Required for *Hairy Kitty Cat Genes*: 50 minutes.

Time Required for *Kitty Cat Toes*: Time will vary depending on the investigation chosen by the student. One class period is probably adequate for most students. You may want to establish a time limit in advance.

Teaching Strategies: Copy the Background Information and the student activity pages for Hairy Kitty Cat Genes and Kitty Cat Toes. Have students read this information and answer the Pre-Lab Questions.

As an introductory activity, ask students what they believe is the probability that their first child will be male. Most students will say 50-50. Show them that they are correct by placing masking tape around a penny. On one side of the penny write an X. On the opposite write a Y. On a second penny covered with masking tape, write an X on both sides. Explain to students that the penny with XX represents the female with her two X chromosomes and that the XY represents the male with one X and one Y chromosome.

To demonstrate fertilization, toss the two coins in the air. When the pennies land, observe the two letters that are facing upward. Record these two letters on the chalkboard as either XX or XY. Repeat this process 19 more times, recording the two resulting letters each time. After 20 tosses, calculate the number of male (XY) and female (XX) children produced. You should find the percentage is close to 50-50. Explain to students that this figure will not always be 50-50 with small numbers of tosses. However, in 100 tosses, it falls very close to a 50-50 percentage.

The partial inquiry lab compares the inheritance of hair length in cats. Short hair is dominant while long hair is recessive in cats. The full inquiry lab deals with five-toed and six-toed cats. Six toes in cats are dominant over five toes.

Evaluation Rubrics

Name _____

Grading Rubric for Hairy Kitty Cat Genes

Criteria	Points Possible	Points Awarded
Pre-Lab Questions correct	35	_____
Data Table correct	30	_____
Post-Lab Questions correct	35	_____
Total	100	_____

Name _____

Grading Rubric for Kitty Cat Toes

Criteria	Points Possible	Points Awarded
Outlined plan for procedure	25	_____
Carried out procedure according to plan	50	_____
Post-Lab Questions correct	25	_____
Total	100	_____

Hairy Kitty Cat Genes
& Kitty Cat Toes

Children receive their genes from their parents. In humans and all other animals, traits are determined by the inheritance of genes. Often you can look at people and see the resemblance between them and their parents. Dark-haired parents often have children with dark hair (Figure 1). Similarly, brown-eyed parents often have children with brown eyes. A short-haired cat often gives birth to short-haired kittens (Figure 2).

Figure 1.

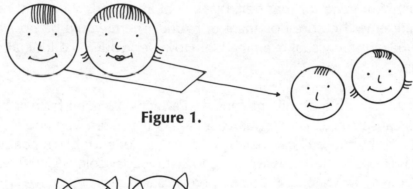

Figure 2.

However, there are cases in which offspring look very different from their parents. Brown-eyed parents can give birth to blue-eyed children, just as short-haired cats can give birth to long-haired kittens (Figure 3). Why don't all offspring look like their parents?

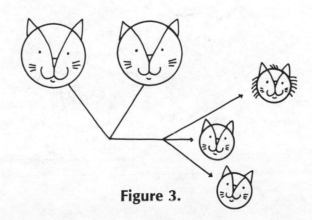

Figure 3.

Many traits in organisms are controlled by two genes. Of these two genes, one is contributed by the mother and the other by the father. When these two genes combine, the trait of the offspring is determined. In this combination of genes, one trait usually dominates over the other one. The presence of a *dominant trait* masks the expression of the *recessive trait*.

A *pure dominant organism* is one that inherited two dominant genes for a trait. For example, If the gene for dark hair is D and the gene for light hair is d, a pure dominant organism has genes DD. A *hybrid organism* has only one dominant gene for that trait. The hybrid's other gene is recessive. The genes in a hybrid are Dd for hair color. A pure recessive organism expresses the recessive trait because it inherited two recessive genes for that trait. The genes in a pure recessive are dd for hair color.

Most of the time, a hybrid and a pure dominant organism look alike because they both express the dominant gene for that trait. Black coat in cattle is dominant over white coat. A black cow could either be pure dominant or hybrid. There would be no way of knowing the cow's genetic makeup by visual examination. However, you could look at its ancestors to get this information.

A hybrid bull carries both a dominant gene and a recessive gene for hair coat color. The dominant gene causes black color. This gene masks the recessive gene for white coat color. During mating, this hybrid bull can pass his dominant gene for black coat color to his offspring, or he can pass the recessive gene for white coat color. A cow with a white coat has two recessive genes for white coat color. She can pass only a recessive white gene to her offspring. If the black bull and the white cow mate, the offspring will inherit a recessive gene for white coat from the mother and will inherit either a dominant or a recessive gene from the father. If the offspring receives the dominant gene from the father, the calf will have a black coat. If it receives a recessive gene from the father, the coat of the calf will be white. See Figure 4.

Figure 4.

Many cats have short hair. In cats, short hair is due to a dominant gene while long hair is due to a recessive gene. The presence or the absence of the gene for short hair determines the hair length in cats.

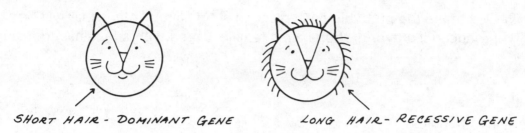

SHORT HAIR - DOMINANT GENE   LONG HAIR - RECESSIVE GENE

Figure 5.

Pre-Lab Questions

1. What is the difference in a pure dominant and a hybrid animal?

_____

_____

2. How many genes govern the expression of most traits?

_____

_____

3. What is the relationship between a dominant and a recessive gene?

_____

_____

4. In cows, if black coat color is dominant over white coat color, can a white bull and a white cow have a black calf? Explain.

_____

Can a black cow and a black bull have a white calf? Explain.

_____

5. Can two long-haired cats have a short-haired kitten? Explain.

_____

_____

Name _____

Hairy Kitty Cat Genes

Purpose: Determine the probable percentage of short-haired kittens that will be produced if a hybrid, short-haired female is bred with a long-haired male.

Materials Needed: Two pennies
Masking tape
Pen

Procedure: 1. Place a small piece of masking tape on both sides of a penny. On one side of the penny write an "S" for the gene for short hair. On the other side of the penny write an "s" for the gene for long hair. This penny represents the genes of a female hybrid short-haired cat. Notice that she has one dominant gene, "S" for short hair. She also has one recessive gene, "s" for long hair (Figure 6).

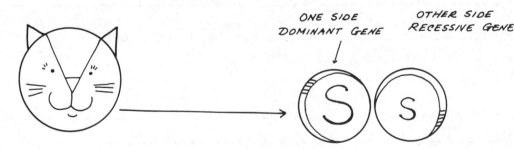

Figure 6.

2. Place a small piece of masking tape on both sides of the second penny. On one side of the penny write an "s" and on the other side also write an "s." This ss combination represents two recessive genes for long hair for the male, long-haired cat in this lab (Figure 7).

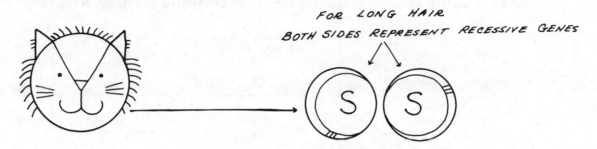

Figure 7.

3. Gently toss these two coins into the air at the same time so that they land on your desk. Tossing pennies represents the actual breeding of the male and female cat. The combination of genes that lands face upward represents the gene combinations for hair length of kittens from these two parents. Record your tosses on the Data Table. Each combination will indicate the hair length of that kitten. For example, if the first toss results in "Ss," check "Ss" in the Data Table for Toss 1. This represents a kitten with short hair because the "S" gene is dominant.

4. Toss the coins and record the genes that are facing upward after Toss 1 in the Data Table.

5. Repeat your toss a total of 49 more times and record the gene combination each time in the Data Table. This represents the female giving birth to 50 kittens over a period of several years. The same male cat is the father of all the kittens.

6. Add the number of "Ss" combinations and enter this total beside "Total" under "Ss." Add the "ss" combinations and enter this total beside "Total" under "ss."

7. Calculate the percentage of "Ss" genes and the percentage of "ss" genes using the formula below. Enter your percentages in the Data Table. The total of the two percentages should equal 100%.

$$\% \text{ offspring with Ss gene} = \frac{\text{Total Ss tosses}}{50} \times 100\%$$

$$\% \text{ offspring with ss gene} = \frac{\text{Total ss tosses}}{50} \times 100\%$$

Data Table. Penny Toss Tallies Representing Kitten Offspring

Toss Number	Ss	ss
1		
2		
3		
4		
5		
6		
7		
8		
9		
10		
11		
12		
13		

14		
15		
16		
17		
18		
19		
20		
21		
22		
23		
24		
25		
26		
27		
28		
29		
30		
31		
32		
33		
34		
35		
36		
37		
38		
39		

40		
41		
42		
43		
44		
45		
46		
47		
48		
49		
50		
Total		
Percentage		

Post-Lab Questions

1. Out of 50 kittens, how many did you determine would have short hair?

_____

2. Why was it not possible to get a pure, short-haired kitten in the 50 kittens?

_____

3. Dominant genes are those that cover the effects of recessive genes. If a cat carries a dominant gene for orange coat color and a recessive gene for black coat color, what color will this animal be? Why?

_____

4. If a pure, short-haired cat is bred with a long-haired cat, predict the percentage of their kittens that will have short hair.

_____

5. How many of the 50 kittens that resulted from this breeding activity are hybrids?

_____

Kitty Cat Toes

A Full Inquiry on Dominant and Recessive Genes

Purpose: Determine the probable percentage of five-toed kittens that will result from breeding a pure six-toed cat and a hybrid six-toed cat?

Materials Needed: _____

_____

_____

_____

Procedure: Design an experiment in which you find the percentage of five-toed kittens produced when a pure six-toed cat is bred with a hybrid six-toed cat. Six toes is dominant to five toes in cats.

Steps in Your Procedure

1. _____

_____

2. _____

_____

3. _____

_____

4. _____

_____

5. _____

_____

Results: Create your own data table if you need one.

_____

_____

_____

Your Data Table

Post-Lab Questions

1. What is the problem that you are trying to solve in this investigation?

   _____
   _____
   _____

2. How did you simulate cat breeding?

   _____
   _____
   _____

3. What percentage of five-toed kittens resulted from this cross?

   _____
   _____
   _____

4. If a hybrid, six-toed cat is mated with a five-toed cat and they produce 20 kittens, how many kittens would you expect to have six toes? Explain your answer.

   _____
   _____
   _____

5. Based on what you learned from this lab, would it be possible for two five-toed cats to produce a six-toed kitten?

   _____
   _____
   _____

4

EARTH & SPACE SCIENCE

Structure of the Earth System

• The solid earth is layered with a lithosphere; hot, convecting mantle; and dense, metallic core.

• Lithospheric plates on the scales of continents and oceans constantly move at rates of centimeters per year in response to movements in the mantle. Major geological events, such as earthquakes, volcanic eruptions, and mountain building result from these plate motions.

• Land forms are the result of a combination of constructive and destructive forces. Constructive forces include crustal deformation, volcanic eruption, and deposition of sediment, while destructive forces include weathering and erosion.

• Some change in the solid earth can be described as the "rock cycle." Old rocks at the earth's surface weather, forming sediments that are buried, then compacted, heated, and often recrystallized into new rock. Eventually, those new rocks may be brought to the surface by the forces that drive plate motions, and the rock cycle continues.

• Soil consists of weathered rocks and decomposed organic material from dead plants, animals, and bacteria. Soils are often found in layers, with each having a different chemical composition and texture.

• Water, which covers most of the earth's surface, circulates through the crust, oceans, and atmosphere in what is known as the "water cycle." Water evaporates from the earth's surface, rises and cools as it moves to higher elevations, condenses as rain or snow, and falls to the surface where it collects in lakes, oceans, soil, and in rocks underground.

• Water is a solvent. As it passes through the water cycle, it dissolves minerals and gases and carries them to the oceans.

• The atmosphere is a mixture of nitrogen, oxygen, and trace gases that include water vapor. The atmosphere has different properties at different elevations.

• Clouds, formed by the condensation of water vapor, affect weather and climate.

- Global patterns of atmospheric movement influence local weather. Oceans have a major effect on climate because water in the oceans holds a large amount of heat.

- Living organisms have played many roles in the earth system, including affecting the composition of the atmosphere, producing some types of rocks, and contributing to the weathering of rocks.

Earth's History
- The earth processes we see today, including erosion, movement of lithospheric plates, and change in atmospheric composition, are similar to those that occurred in the past. Earth history is also influenced by occasional catastrophes, such as the impact of an asteroid or comet.

- Fossils provide important evidence of how life and environmental conditions have changed.

Earth in the Solar System
- The earth is the third planet from the sun in a system that includes the moon, the sun, eight other planets and their moons, and smaller objects, such as asteroids and comets. The sun, an average star, is the central and largest body in the solar system.

- Most objects in the solar system are in regular and predictable motion. Those motions explain such phenomena as the day, the year, phases of the moon, and eclipses.

- Gravity is the force that keeps planets in orbit around the sun and governs the rest of the motion in the solar system. Gravity alone holds us to the earth's surface and explains the phenomena of the tides.

- The sun is the major source of energy for phenomena on the earth's surface, such as growth of plants, winds, ocean currents, and the water cycle. Seasons result from variations in the amount of the sun's energy hitting the surface, due to the tilt of the earth's rotation on its axis and the length of the day.

The Chemical Breakdown of Rocks & The Physical Breakdown of Rocks

Teacher Information

NSTA
Objectives: Land forms are the result of a combination of constructive and destructive forces. Constructive forces include crustal deformation, volcanic eruption, and deposition of sediment, while destructive forces include weathering and erosion.

Soil consists of weathered rocks and decomposed organic material from dead plants, animals, and bacteria. Soils are often found in layers, with each having a different chemical composition and texture.

Specific
Objectives: Students will observe the effects of chemical weathering on different types of rocks.

Students will observe the effects of physical weathering on different types of rocks.

Time
Required for *The Chemical Breakdown of Rocks*: Day 1—40 minutes
Day 2—20 minutes
Day 3—40 minutes

Time
Required for *The Physical Breakdown of Rocks*:

Time requirements will vary depending on the investigation the student chooses. If you allow part of the class period for two days, this should be adequate. You may want to set a time limit on student investigations.

Teaching
Strategies: Copy the Background Information and the student activity pages for The Chemical Breakdown of Rocks and The Physical Breakdown of Rocks. Have students read this information and answer the Pre-Lab Questions.

Caution students that safety glasses should be worn for these investigations.

As an introductory activity, weigh a piece of limestone and write its mass on the board. Using a dropper, add about 30 ml of 6 M* (molar) hydrochloric acid to the limestone. (See directions below for preparing acid.) Wait about five minutes, pour off the acid, dry the limestone with a paper towel, and reweigh the limestone.

Write the new mass on the board. Ask students why there was a change in mass. Use this opportunity to relate the limestone and acid in this demonstration to the formation of limestone caves by carbonic acid. Carbonic acid forms as carbon dioxide in air mixes with rainwater.

Water + carbon dioxide $\longrightarrow$ carbonic acid

$$H_2O + CO_2 \longrightarrow H_2CO_3$$

Weathering can alter the appearance of large rocks and some man-made structures. Some rocks weather more easily than others.

In the partial inquiry, acid represents the chemical weathering agent. Different types of rocks are used so that students can evaluate the rate at which different rock types weather. The full inquiry lab allows students to evaluate the effects of physical weathering on rock types.

A 3 M solution of hydrochloric acid is needed in the partial inquiry.

Molarity is a way of expressing the concentration of a solution.
*To dilute acids, use the formula:
$$M_cV_c = M_dV_d$$
where M_c = molarity of concentrated acid
M_d = molarity of diluted acid
V_c = volume of concentrated acid
V_d = volume of diluted acid
To prepare 250 ml of 6 M HCL from 9 M (muriatic acid), dilute 167 ml of acid with water to a total volume of 250 ml.

To prepare 1 liter of 3 M HCL from 9 M, dilute 333 ml of acid with water to a total volume of 1 liter.

To prepare 1 liter of 3 M HCL from 12 M (concentrated lab grade) HCL, dilute 250 ml of acid with water to 1 liter.

Caution: Always dilute acids by pouring acid down a stirring rod into a beaker of water. Wear goggles and work in a well-ventilated area.

Students should wear safety glasses in the lab. Prior to the lab, caution the class about the possible dangers of acid burns. If students get acid on their skin or in their eyes, they should wash the area with water immediately and contact the teacher.

Evaluation Rubrics

Name _____

Grading Rubric for The Chemical Breakdown of Rocks

Criteria	Points Possible	Points Awarded
Pre-Lab Questions correct	35	_____
Data Table correct	30	_____
Post-Lab Questions correct	35	_____
Total	100	_____

Name _____

Grading Rubric for The Physical Breakdown of Rocks

Criteria	Points Possible	Points Awarded
Listed materials	15	_____
Outlined plan for procedure	15	_____
Carried out procedure	30	_____
Post-Lab Questions correct	40	_____
Total	100	_____

The Chemical Breakdown of Rocks

& The Physical Breakdown of Rocks

On earth, rocks are exposed to the forces of nature. Water, wind, chemicals, and agents in the atmosphere can cause rocks to change appearance. The breaking down and wearing away of rocks is called *weathering*. Weathering can be classified as either chemical or physical.

In *physical weathering,* rocks are broken into smaller pieces. Physical weathering can be caused by wind, water, and plants. The sand and debris carried by a strong wind can break rock into smaller pieces. The roots of large trees often crack and weaken rocks (Figure 1). Even strong currents of water flowing over rocks can cause physical weathering.

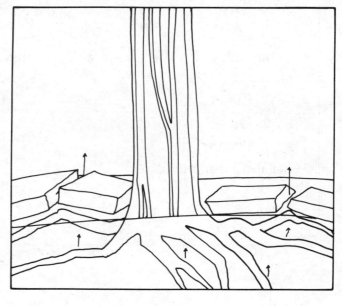

Figure 1.

To see physical weathering, half-fill a jar with water. Place soft rocks such as sandstone or chalk in the jar, cap it, and shake for five minutes (see Figure 2). The action of the water on the rocks breaks them into smaller pieces. This is an example of physical weathering.

SHAKE!

Figure 2.

Chemical weathering changes not only the size of rocks but also the material that makes up the rocks. One place where chemical weathering occurs is in limestone caves. In the air, carbon dioxide mixes with water vapor to form carbonic acid. This weak acid reacts with the minerals in the limestone. As limestone dissolves over the years, caves change in appearance.

Not all rocks weather at the same rate. The rate of weathering is affected by the type of rock and the minerals that make up that rock. Climate can also affect the rate of weathering. Rocks that are composed of water-soluble minerals weather more rapidly than rocks that are not water soluble. Rocks that react with acids also weather more quickly than rocks that are not affected by acids.

There are three types of rocks: *sedimentary, metamorphic,* and *igneous.* The most common type of rock is *sedimentary rock.* This type is formed from sediment that is brought to an area by the forces of erosion. These sediments are deposited in layers. Over time, the layers of sediment are pressed together by the forces of nature. The minerals in these layers are cemented by slow, intensive pressure (see Figure 3).

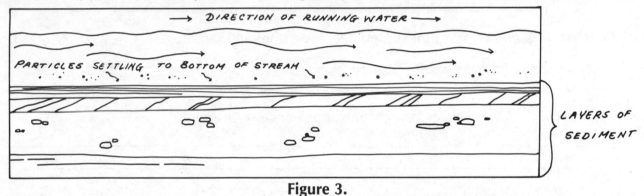

Figure 3.

Sedimentary rocks can be made from different substances, such as limestone or clay. A cementing mineral fills the spaces between the grains of clay or limestone to hold it in place. Water can penetrate sedimentary rocks by dissolving the material that cements these rocks together. For this reason, sedimentary rocks weather quickly.

Common types of sedimentary rock include:
    a. shale, which is made of particles of mud and clay,
    b. sandstone, which is formed when particles of sand are pressed together,
    c. limestone, made from particles of calcium carbonate or from the shells of sea animals.

Metamorphic rock is created when sedimentary or igneous rocks are chemically changed. Hot, liquid rock deep inside the earth causes a chemical reaction with existing rocks. New materials, called *metamorphic rocks,* are formed during these chemical reactions. Marble and granite are examples of metamorphic rock.

Igneous rock is formed from hot, molten magma deep in the earth. This magma is forced to or near the surface where it cools and hardens. Lava is one type of igneous rock.

Climate also influences rock weathering. The more precipitation there is in an area, the more rapidly weathering occurs. Weathering is very common in humid climates that experience a wide range of temperatures. Pollutants in the air can also react chemically with rocks to increase the rate of weathering.

Pre-Lab Questions

1. Define *weathering*.

_____

_____

2. What is the difference between physical and chemical weathering?

_____

_____

3. What makes some rocks more susceptible to weathering than others?

_____

_____

4. Explain how limestone caves can change appearance over time.

_____

_____

5. How can climate affect the rate of weathering?

_____

_____

6. Is strong wind blowing on rocks an example of chemical or physical weathering? Defend your answer.

_____

_____

The Chemical Breakdown of Rocks

A Partial Inquiry on Chemical Weathering of Rocks

Purpose: Observe the effects of chemical weathering on different types of rocks.

**Materials
Needed:** Marble pieces
Granite pieces
Limestone pieces
Triple beam balance
Paper towels
Water
3 M hydrochloric acid
Three 250-ml beakers
One 1,000-ml beaker (optional)
Wire screen
Water faucet
Safety glasses

Procedure: 1. Label the beakers as A, B, and C.

2. Fill beakers to the 100-ml mark with rock fragments as follows:

   Beaker A—Marble
   Beaker B—Granite
   Beaker C—Limestone

3. Rinse the rocks in each beaker to get rid of any dirt particles that may still be attached to the rocks. Repeat the rinse several times. As you pour the water from the beaker, place a wire gauze or screen over the beaker so the rocks do not fall out of the beaker (Figure 4).

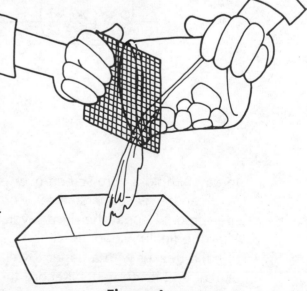

Figure 4.

4. Once all the beakers of rocks have been washed and emptied of water, dry the inside and outside of the beakers with a paper towel. Use a triple beam balance to find the mass of each beaker and its contents. Record the mass of each beaker and its contents in the Data Table under the column "Mass of Beaker and Contents at Start."

Safety glasses should be worn from this point to the end of the lab.

5. Pour 3M hydrochloric acid into each beaker so that the rocks are submerged in acid.

Hydrochloric acid can cause burns to the skin and eyes. If you get this acid on your skin or in your eyes, wash the exposed area with water immediately and notify your teacher.

6. Set the three beakers aside until the next day (Figure 5).

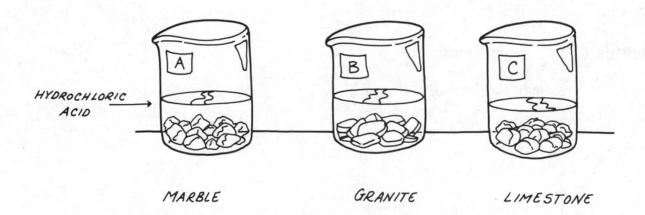

HYDROCHLORIC ACID →

MARBLE   GRANITE   LIMESTONE

Figure 5.

7. On day 2, hold a wire screen over each beaker as you pour the acid into a large beaker. (Acid can be reused in step #9.) Rinse the rocks with water. Pour off the water using the wire screen. Repeat the rinse several times.
8. After the final rinse, drain all the water from each beaker and wipe the inside and outside of each beaker with a paper towel. Use the triple beam balance to find the mass of each beaker and its contents. Record this information in the Data Table under the column "Mass of Beaker and Contents on Day 2."

9. Add enough 3M hydrochloric acid to each beaker so the rocks in each beaker are once again submerged. Set the beakers aside for 48 hours.

10. On Day 4, use a wire screen to pour the acid from each beaker. Rinse the contents of the beaker several times with water. Wipe the inside and outside of each beaker with a paper towel and use a triple beam balance to obtain the mass of each beaker and its contents. Record this in the Data Table under "Mass of beaker and contents on Day 4."

Data Table. Mass of Beakers and Their Contents

	Mass of Beaker and Contents at Start	Mass of Beaker and Contents on Day 2	Mass of Beaker and Contents on Day 4
Beaker A			
Beaker B			
Beaker C			

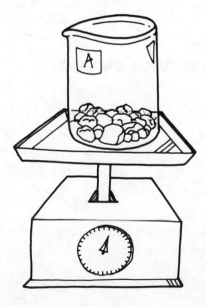

Post-Lab Questions

1. Which beaker showed the greatest change in mass over the four days? Which showed the least change in mass?

_____

_____

2. Explain how your experimental results and weathering are related.

_____

_____

3. Explain how the mass of the rocks was affected as the number of days of exposure increased.

_____

_____

4. Explain why this lab demonstrates chemical rather than physical weathering.

_____

_____

5. Explain why using a wire screen was important to your results in this lab.

_____

_____

6. Which do you think would best resist deterioration, a statue made of sandstone or a statue made of granite? Explain your answer.

_____

_____

The Physical Breakdown of Rocks

Purpose: Observe the effects of physical weathering on different types of rocks.

**Materials
Needed:** _____

_____

_____

_____

Procedure: Design an experiment in which you measure the effect of physical weathering on different types of rocks.

Steps in Your Procedure

1. _____

_____

2. _____

_____

3. _____

_____

4. _____

_____

5. _____

_____

Results: Create your own data table if you need one.

_____

_____

_____

Your Data Table

Post-Lab Questions

1. What is the problem that you are trying to solve in this investigation?

   _____

   _____

2. What was the variable in this investigation?

   _____

   _____

3. How did you simulate physical weathering?

   _____

   _____

4. Which rock type seemed to be most affected by physical weathering?

   _____

   _____

5. How is physical weathering different from chemical weathering?

   _____

   _____

6. Explain why it would be unwise to build structures out of sandstone in areas of strong winds.

   _____

   _____

Water on the Run & Close Knit

NSTA
Objectives: Soil consists of weathered rocks and decomposed organic material from dead plants, animals, and bacteria. Soils are often found in layers, with each having a different chemical composition and texture.

Specific
Objectives: Students will determine how soil texture, particle size, and packing of the soil affect soil permeability.

Time
Required for *Water on the Run*: 50 minutes

Time
Required for *Close Knit*: Time will vary according to the investigation chosen by the student. Most students should be able to complete the activity in one or two class periods. You may want to set some time limits for this investigation.

Teaching
Strategies: Copy the Background Information and the student activity pages for Water on the Run and Close Knit. Have students read this information and complete the Pre-Lab Questions.

As an introductory activity, fill a 100-ml graduated cylinder half full of sand. Ask students if they think the volume of material in the cup will increase if they pour water into the cylinder. Slowly pour some water into the cylinder. The water should seep into the soil without raising the volume, demonstrating a process called *infiltration*. As water seeps into the sand, it occupies the spaces between the particles of sand.

Fill a glass partially full of marbles. Students should observe that there are spaces between the marbles. Explain that the marbles represent individual particles of sand. Water seeps into spaces between particles of sand when it infiltrates soil. Describe the spaces between particles as *pores*.

In the partial inquiry, small, medium, and large particles are needed. Clay can represent the small particles, aquarium gravel or coarse sand can be used for medium particles, and large gravel or marble chips can be used for large particles.

Save empty, two-liter soda bottles for these activities. The day before the lab, use an ice pick to punch holes in the caps of each bottle so that water can drain when the bottles are used in the funnel apparatus.

Evaluation Rubrics

Name _____

Grading Rubric for Water on the Run

Criteria	Points Possible	Points Awarded
Pre-Lab Questions correct	35	_____
Data Table completed correctly	30	_____
Post-Lab Questions correct	35	_____
Total	100	_____

Name _____

Grading Rubric for Close Knit

Criteria	Points Possible	Points Awarded
Materials listed	15	_____
Outlined plan for experiment	15	_____
Carried out procedure according to plan	50	_____
Post-Lab Questions correct	20	_____
Total	100	_____

Water on the Run

Close Knit

On earth, freshwater can be divided into three types, based on where it is found:
  a. frozen water,
  b. ground water,
  c. surface water.

Most freshwater is located in glaciers and polar ice caps. The second largest class of fresh water is located in the ground. There is much more fresh water in the ground than in all the rivers, streams, ponds, and other surface waters on earth.

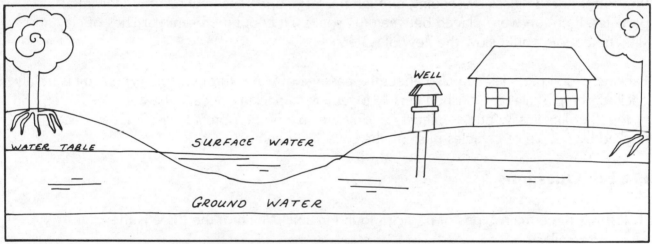

Figure 1. Most of the liquid fresh water is ground water.

Water enters the ground through openings or spaces in the soil by the process of *infiltration*. The material composing the soil influences how much water can infiltrate that soil. Different places on earth have different types and textures of soil. Some soil is sandy, some is rocky, some is full of gravel, and some is a combination of many textures.

The size of soil particles determines the size of pore spaces between particles. The larger the pore spaces, the easier it is for water to flow through the soil. The amount of water that seeps into soil depends on the number and size of pore spaces and whether the spaces are connected.

Many soils contain particles of sand, clay, and silt. Clay particles are the smallest. They are flat and irregular in shape. As a general rule, clay has a low *permeability*. That means that water does not penetrate clay soil very well. Sand particles, which are larger than clay particles, are round and smooth. Silt particles are larger than clay, but smaller than sand (Figure 2). As a general rule, sand and silt are much more permeable than clay.

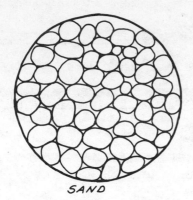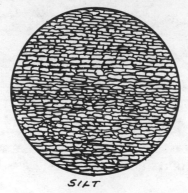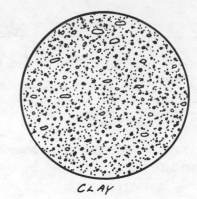

SAND   SILT   CLAY

Figure 2.

Most soils are made of a combination of sand, silt, and clay particles. The smaller silt and clay particles sometimes fill the large pores between sand particles. They clog these openings and cause water to pass slowly through the soil. To visualize this concept, think about the glass full of marbles that represent sand particles. Water that is poured into this glass flows quickly to the bottom of the glass by seeping through the large openings between the individual particles. If cotton were placed between the spaces, it could represent particles of clay and silt. The cotton would slow the flow of water.

Packing of soil particles can also affect the passage of water through soil. When soil is tightly packed, the particles are pushed closely together. As packing occurs, the particles flatten and fit together like jigsaw puzzle pieces, closing the size of the pore spaces. Soil can become packed by people or vehicles pushing the particles together.

Pre-Lab Questions

1. List the three main types of particles found in soil. Which of the three is the largest? Which is the smallest?

   _____

   _____

2. Rank the three soil particles according to permeability. Rank the most permeable as 1 and the least permeable as 3.

   _____

   _____

3. Define *permeability*.

   _____

   _____

4. Define *infiltration*.

   _____

   _____

5. What other factors, besides soil size, affect permeability of the soil?

   _____

   _____

Water on the Run

Purpose: Determine how texture and particle size affect soil permeability.

**Materials
Needed:** Two empty, 2-liter plastic soft drink bottles with caps containing several holes
Scissors
Aquarium gravel or very coarse sand
Marble chips or large pieces of gravel
Clay
Graduated cylinder
Spoon
Watch with a second hand
Water
250-ml beaker

Procedure: 1. Convert your soft drink bottle to a funnel by cutting it in half with scissors. Place the cap filled with holes on the mouth of the bottle. Invert the top half of the bottle, mouth downward, into the bottom half. (Figure 3)

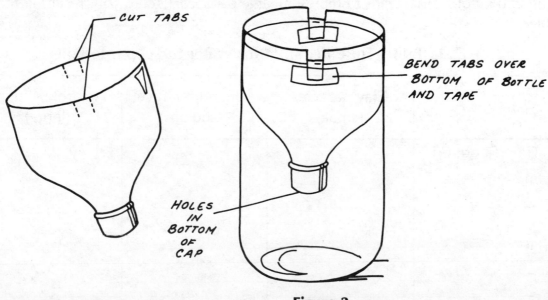

CUT TABS

BEND TABS OVER
BOTTOM OF BOTTLE
AND TAPE

HOLES
IN
BOTTOM
OF
CAP

Figure 3.

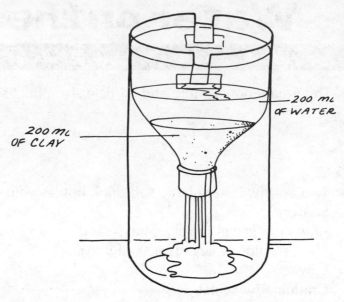

200 ml OF WATER

200 ml OF CLAY

2. Use a beaker to measure 200 ml of clay.

Figure 4.

3. Transfer the clay from the beaker into the funnel. Measure 200 ml of water and pour it on top of the clay in the funnel (Figure 4).

4. Time how long it takes for the water to drain through the clay, until it is level with the top of the clay. Record this time in the Data Table.

5. Remove the clay from the funnel and wash the funnel and cap. Repeat steps 2 through 4 using 200 ml of aquarium gravel to represent your medium-sized particles. Record your results in the Data Table.

6. Remove the aquarium gravel and wash the funnel and cap. Repeat Steps 2 through 4 using 200 ml of marble chips to represent large particles. Record your results in the Data Table.

Data Table. Time Required for Water to Seep into Soil

	Clay Particles (small)	Aquarium Gravel (medium)	Marble Chips (large)
Time Required			

Post-Lab Questions

1. Through which particles did water pass the most quickly? the most slowly?

   _____

   _____

2. Would you expect rain to form puddles in sand, silt, or clay? Why?

   _____

   _____

3. Explain why you might hesitate to plant crops in a soil made of pure clay.

   _____

   _____

4. Which would be least likely to erode quickly—sand, silt, or clay particles?

   _____

   _____

5. Explain how particle size is related to permeability of water.

   _____

   _____

6. You have a soil sample that is 75 ml of clay, 75 ml of sand, and 75 ml of silt. If you place the sample in the funnel and add 225 ml of water, predict how fast water can pass through and into the soil, based on the results you obtained in lab today.

   _____

   _____

Name _____

Close Knit

Purpose: Determine how packing of soil affects permeability.

Materials Needed: _____
_____
_____
_____

Procedure: Design an experiment in which you measure the effect that pressing soil particles closely together (packing them) has on the ability of water to penetrate the soil.

Steps in Your Procedure

1. _____
_____

2. _____
_____

3. _____
_____

4. _____
_____

5. _____
_____

Results: Create your own data table if you need one.

_____
_____
_____

Your Data Table

Post-Lab Questions

1. What is the problem that you are trying to solve in this investigation?

   _____

   _____

2. What effect did packing the soil have on its permeability?

   _____

   _____

3. How does packing soil affect its pore size?

   _____

   _____

4. Use the information gathered from this lab to explain why walking across soil that has been recently planted with grass seeds may affect the growth of the seedlings.

   _____

   _____

5. Based on the information in this lab, explain why the rangers in national forests request that visitors stay on nature trails.

   _____

   _____

SCIENCE & TECHNOLOGY

Identify appropriate problems for technological design.

Design a solution or product.

Implement a proposed design.

Evaluate completed technological designs or products.

Communicate the process of technological design.

Understandings About Science and Technology
- Scientific inquiry and technological design have similarities and differences. Scientists propose explanations for questions about the natural world, and engineers propose solutions relating to human problems, needs, and aspirations. Technological solutions are temporary; technologies exist within nature, and so they cannot contravene physical or biological principles; technological solutions have side effects; and technologies have costs, carry risks, and provide benefits.

- Many different people in different cultures have made and continue to make contributions to science and technology.

- Science and technology are reciprocal. Science helps drive technology, as it addresses questions that demand more sophisticated instruments and provides principles for better instrumentation and technique. Technology is essential to science, because it provides instruments and techniques that enable observations of objects and phenomena that are otherwise unobservable due to factors such as quantity, distance, location, size, and speed. Technology also provides tools for investigations, inquiry, and analysis.

- Perfectly designed solutions do not exist. All technological solutions have tradeoffs, such as safety, cost, efficiency, and appearance. Engineers often build back-up systems to provide safety. Risk is part of living in a highly technological world. Reducing risk often results in new technology.

- Technological designs have constraints. Some constraints are unavoidable, for example, properties of materials or effects of weather and friction; other constraints limit choices in the design, for example, environmental protection, human safety, and aesthetics.

- Technological solutions have intended benefits and unintended consequences.

- Some consequences can be predicted; others cannot.

A Unique Design & My Creative Side

Teacher Information

NSTA

Objectives: Design a solution or a product.

Implement a proposed design.

Communicate the process of technological design.

Specific

Objectives: Students design a miniature boat that can support 500 grams of weight.

Students design a new product and present it to the class.

Time

Required for *A Unique Design*: Day 1—20 minutes
Day 2—50 minutes
Day 3—30 minutes

Time

Required for *My Creative Side*: Varies with each student design; you might want to set limitations on how much time students can spend on this investigation.

Teaching

Strategies: Copy Background Information and student activity pages for the students. Have them read the Background Information on A Unique Design and My Creative Side and answer the Pre-Lab Questions.

As an introductory activity, show students several different toy boats. Ask students why speed boats and barges have different designs.

For both the partial inquiry, A Unique Design, and the full inquiry, My Creative Side, make a large box of art supplies and usable "junk" available to students. Paper plates, pie plates, aluminum foil, empty plastic bottles, string, yarn, cardboard, and plenty of other materials should be available so that students can have every opportunity to be creative.

Evaluation Rubrics

Name _____

Grading Rubric for A Unique Design

Criteria	Points Possible	Points Awarded
Boat designed and materials listed before assembly	20	_____
Boat held 500 grams	20	_____
Boat was attractive	10	_____
Presentation:		
is interesting	10	_____
lasts 1-2 minutes	10	_____
uses props/costumes/visual aids	10	_____
Pre- and Post-Lab Questions correct	20	_____
Total	100	_____

Name _____

Grading Rubric for My Creative Side

Criteria	Points Possible	Points Awarded
Outlined plan for product	25	_____
Assembled product according to plan	25	_____
Presented product to class:		
in interesting manner	10	_____
presentation lasted 1-2 minutes	05	_____
props/costumes/visual aids used	10	_____
Wrote steps for Procedure and answered Post-Lab Questions	25	_____
Total	100	_____

A Unique Design

& My Creative Side

You may have noticed that it is easier to pick up your friend in a swimming pool than it is when you are not in the pool. People and objects are pulled toward the earth by gravity, a force that gives them weight. In water, some of the downward force of gravity is counterbalanced by an upward force called *buoyancy*. In the pool, some of your friend's weight is supported by buoyancy.

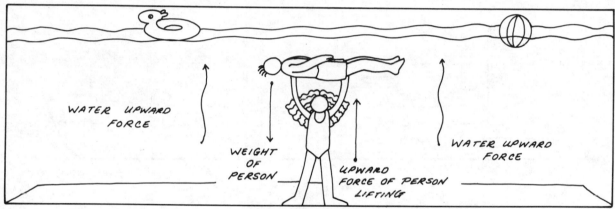

Figure 1.

When you sit in a bathtub of water, the water level rises. The water level changes because your body moves aside, or displaces, some of the water. The weight of the water that you move aside is equal to the buoyant force with which the water pushes against you.

The amount of the buoyant force against an object determines whether that object will float or sink in a fluid. An object will float if the buoyant force is equal to or greater than that object's weight. However, if the buoyant force is less than that object's weight, the object will sink (Figure 2).

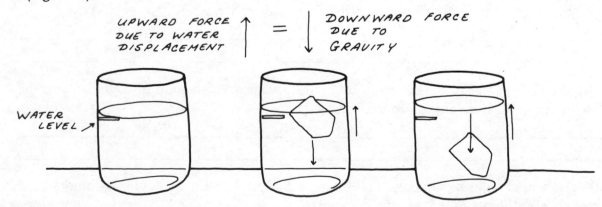

Figure 2. The downward force on a floating object due to gravity will be equal to the upward force due to water displacement. When an object is added to a container of water, the water level rises.

Dense materials are more likely to sink in water than materials that are not dense. Air is not as dense as water, and floats above it. Oil is another substance that floats on water. Metals, which are much more dense than water, usually sink. However, most ships are made of metals.

When you think about a ship, you realize that it is not solid metal. Ships are actually a combination of metals and air because they are hollow inside. The metal in a ship plus the air associated with it have an average density that is less than that of water's. The ship and air displace a weight of water that is equal to or greater than the weight of the ship. Therefore, the ship floats.

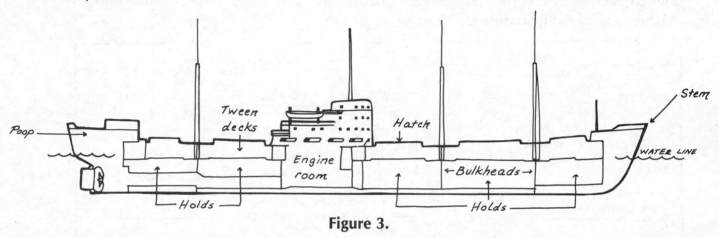

Figure 3.

Pre-Lab Questions

1. What is *buoyancy*?

   _____

   _____

2. If you get into a bathtub that is filled to the brim with water, what happens? Why?

   _____

   _____

3. You float higher in salt water than you do in fresh water. Which type of water do you think exerts the greatest buoyant force, fresh or salt?

   _____

   _____

4. A 500-gram steel ball sinks in water. However, if that 500 grams of steel is hammered into a bowl shape, it floats in water. Why?

   _____

   _____

A Unique Design

A Partial Inquiry on Product Design

Purpose: Design a miniature boat that can support 500 grams of weight.

Materials Needed: Art supplies such as glue, scissors, cardboard, paint, crayons, string, tape, fabric, aluminum foil, etc.
Weights (nuts, bolts, nails, coins, or anything heavy)
A pail of water

Procedure Day 1:

1. Design a small boat that can support at least 500 grams.

2. The boat must not exceed a size of 16 cm by 10 cm.

3. Sketch the design for your boat below. List the materials you plan to use to construct your boat.

4. Your boat must be attractive.

Sketch of my boat:

Materials needed to build my boat:

Procedure Day 2: 5. Assemble the materials that you need to construct your boat, then build it.

6. Test your boat's ability to hold 500 grams by placing it in the pail of water and adding the test weights.

7. Submit your boat to your teacher, or his/her appointed helper, for evaluation.

Procedure Day 3: 8. Design a TV commercial about your boat to describe it to your classmates.

9. Your commercial should be 1 to 2 minutes long. You may enlist the help of other students, if you wish.

Your commercial should show your model, and explain why the boat made from this model does a great job of supporting 500 grams. In your commercial, use props, costumes, or other visual aids.

Be clever, imaginative, and exciting so that the rest of the class will enjoy hearing about your work. Seek to entertain and to educate your classmates.

Post-Lab Questions

1. Describe the design of the boat that held the most weight.

_____

_____

2. Why was it important to design your boat before you started building it?

_____

_____

3. The following two boats are built with the same amount of aluminum. Which do you think could carry the most weight? Why?

_____

_____

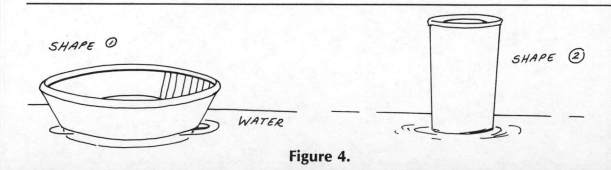

Figure 4.

My Creative Side

A Full Inquiry on Product Design

Purpose: Identify an appropriate product for you to design.

Design your product.

Present your product to your classmates.

Procedure: Outline your plans for identifying a product that you can design, designing that product, and presenting that product to the class in an interesting and informative way. Then identify, design, assemble, and present that product to class.

Steps in Your Procedure

1. _____
   _____

2. _____
   _____

3. _____
   _____

4. _____
   _____

5. _____
   _____

Place the sketch of the product you plan to make and the materials needed to make that product in the box below.

Sketch:

Materials:

Outline for Telling Others About Your Product

Post-Lab Questions

1. What is the purpose of this investigation?

   _____

   _____

2. Would you have designed a different product if more materials had been made available? What materials would you have liked to have? What product would you have made?

   _____

   _____

3. In your opinion, what was the most difficult task in designing, constructing, and advertising a product?

   _____

   _____

4. Someone once said that there is nothing left to invent "because everything has already been invented." Do you agree or disagree with this comment? Explain your answer.

   _____

   _____

Pretty Bubbles & Oldest Bubbles

Teacher Information

NSTA
Objectives: Students should use criteria relevant to the original purpose or need, consider a variety of factors that might affect acceptability and suitability for intended users or beneficiaries, and develop measures of quality with respect to such criteria and factors; they should also suggest improvements and, for their own products, try proposed modifications.

Specific
Objectives: Students will design bubble recipes that produce bubbles with long life spans.

Time
Required for *Pretty Bubbles:* 1 hour

Time
Required for *Oldest Bubbles:* About 1 hour; varies according to student designs.

Teaching
Strategies: Copy Background Information and student activity pages for students. Have them read the background information on Pretty Bubbles and Oldest Bubbles and answer the questions.

As an introductory activity, bring a commercial bubble-blowing mixture to school and let students try it. Have students count the number of bubbles they can blow from one "scoop" of bubble mixture. Also, have them time several of their bubbles to see how long it takes them to burst. Students can use these times to determine the average life span of bubbles made from commercial bubble solution.

Evaluation Rubrics

Name _____

Grading Rubric for Pretty Bubbles

Criteria	Points Possible	Points Awarded
Pre-Lab Questions correct	33	_____
Completed Data Table	34	_____
Post-Lab Questions correct	33	_____
Total	100	_____

Name _____

Grading Rubric for Oldest Bubbles

Criteria	Points Possible	Points Awarded
Listed materials	25	_____
Wrote steps for Procedure	25	_____
Created appropriate Data Table	25	_____
Post-Lab Questions correct	25	_____
Total	100	_____

Pretty Bubbles

Oldest Bubbles

Bubbles are composed of air inside a hollow liquid ball. Soap bubbles, like those that form in the bath water, are pockets of air inside a film of soapy water. Soap bubbles are held together by water's surface tension. Water molecules are attracted to one another. The water molecules are much more attracted to one another than they are to the air molecules. It is very difficult to make a bubble out of plain water because the water molecules are held together so tightly that you cannot separate them to form a pocket of air. If you add soap to the water, you reduce the surface tension of the water so that the molecules do not hold on to one another as tightly as before. This allows bubbles to form.

Once you form a bubble, it usually does not last long before it bursts. Water evaporates quickly and this causes the wall of the bubble to break. Bubbles that last for a long time before popping usually have something added to the soap and water mixture to slow evaporation of water. Glycerine is one substance that slows evaporation of water. It does so because this liquid forms a chemical bond in water that delays evaporation. In other words, the addition of glycerine to the bubble mixture makes the bubble stronger and last longer. However, the amount of glycerine you add to a bubble recipe is important. Too much glycerine makes the bubble mixture heavy and prevents the formation of bubbles. Too little glycerine does not extend the life of the bubbles. Glycerine is a thick, colorless, odorless liquid that has a slightly sweet taste. It prevents the evaporation of water from materials. Glycerine is used commercially to keep products such as make-up and fruit moist.

Soap bubbles have been the playthings of children for generations. You can find soap bubble recipes in many different books. All soap bubble recipes are very similar. Two common recipes are:

Recipe A: 1 to 3 parts liquid dishwashing detergent + 6 parts water

Recipe B: 1 to 3 parts liquid dishwashing detergent + 6 parts water + 1 to 4 parts glycerine

Pre-Lab Questions

1. What are three common ingredients found in soap bubbles?

_____

_____

2. Explain the role of glycerine in increasing bubble life span.

_____

_____

3. What is the purpose of adding soap to water when making bubbles?

_____

_____

4. Why is the amount of glycerine used in bubble recipes important?

_____

_____

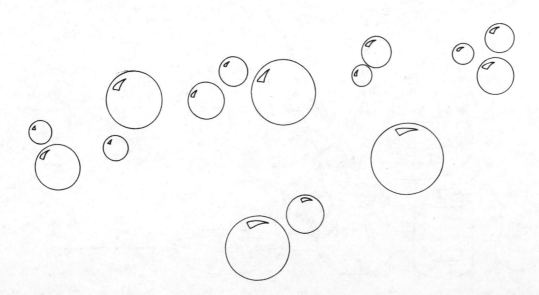

Pretty Bubbles

A Partial Inquiry on Soap Bubble Recipes

Purpose: Students will design bubble recipes using various amounts of glycerine to determine the amount that produces the longest-lasting bubbles.

Materials Needed:
Four beakers or jars
Graduated cylinder
Liquid dishwashing detergent
Glycerine
Warm water
Coat hanger
Watch or clock with second hand
Grease pen or labels

Procedure:
1. Label the beakers as A, B, C, and D.

2. To all four beakers, add 15 ml of liquid dishwashing detergent and 120 ml of warm water.

3. To beaker A, do not add any glycerine. Beaker A is the control in this experiment.

4. To beaker B add 7 ml of glycerine.

5. To beaker C add 15 ml of glycerine.

6. To beaker D add 30 ml of glycerine. Stir the contents of each beaker gently (see Figure 1).

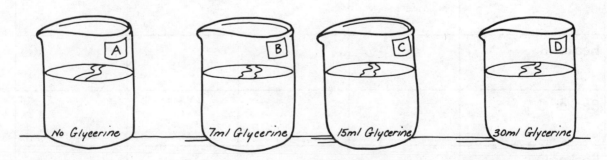

Figure 1.

7. Unwrap a coat hanger so that it is one long piece of wire. Bend the end of it into a loop about an inch in diameter (Figure 2). Dip the loop into beaker A, and wave it through the air to form a bubble. Use a clock with a second hand to time how long the bubble floats in the air before bursting. Enter this time in the Data Table beside "Beaker A."

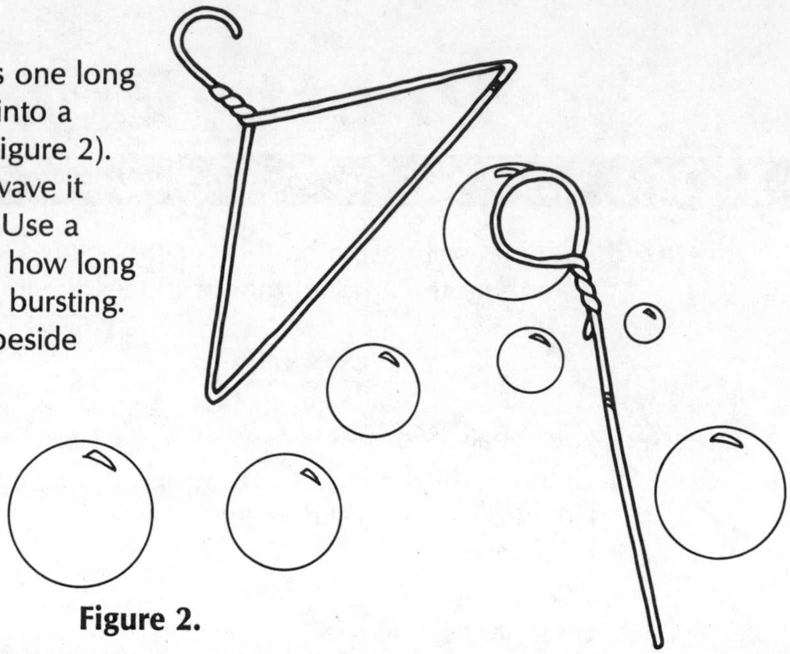

Figure 2.

Repeat this procedure two more times in beaker A, and record all the times from all three trials in the Data Table. Add all three times from beaker A, then divide the total time by 3 to get an average time. Enter the average time in the Data Table.

8. Dip the coat hanger loop into beaker B, wave it through the air to form a bubble, and time how long the bubble floats before breaking. Enter the time in the Data Table beside "Beaker B."

Repeat this procedure twice with beaker B and record your data in the Data Table. Add the times from all three trials from beaker B, then divide the total time by 3 to get an average time. Enter the average time in the Data Table.

9. Repeat step #8 for beakers C and D.

Data Table

Time Bubble Lasted Before Bursting	Trial 1	Trial 2	Trial 3	Average of All Three Trials
Beaker A				
Beaker B				
Beaker C				
Beaker D				

Post-Lab Questions

1. What is the problem that you are trying to solve in this investigation?

_____

_____

2. What is the variable in this experiment?

_____

_____

3. What is the control in this experiment?

_____

_____

4. Which recipe for soap bubbles produced the longest-lasting bubbles?

_____

_____

5. If you worked for a toy manufacturer, recommend your bubble recipe. Explain your recommendations to the manufacturer.

_____

_____

Oldest Bubbles

A Full Inquiry on Soap Bubble Recipes

Purpose: Students will design bubble recipes using various amounts of detergent to determine the amount that produces the longest-lasting bubbles.

Materials Needed: _____

_____

_____

_____

Procedure: Design an experiment in which you vary the amount of dishwashing detergent in a bubble recipe. Determine how various amounts of the dishwashing detergent affect the life span of the bubbles.

Steps in Your Procedure

1. _____

_____

2. _____

_____

3. _____

_____

4. _____

_____

5. _____

_____

Results: Create your own data table if you need one.

_____

_____

_____

Your Data Table

Post-Lab Questions

1. What is the ideal amount of dishwashing detergent in a bubble recipe?

_____

_____

2. How long did the bubbles from this recipe last before they burst?

_____

_____

3. What is the variable in your experiment?

_____

_____

4. What is the control in your experiment?

_____

_____

5. Did you list any materials that you did not need? Explain why you listed those materials.

_____

_____

6. Explain how you might design an experiment to test the following hypothesis: Bubbles made in cold water have a longer life span than bubbles made in warm water.

_____

_____

7. Write a six-sentence, commercial message that advertises the bubble recipe that you found to be superior to the other recipes in producing bubbles that last a long time.

_____

_____

_____

_____

SCIENCE IN PERSONAL & SOCIAL PERSPECTIVES

Personal Health

• Regular exercise is important to the maintenance and improvement of health. The benefits of physical fitness include maintaining healthy weight, having strength for routine activities, good muscle tone, bone strength, strong heart/lung systems, and improved mental health. Personal exercise, especially developing cardiovascular endurance, is the foundation of physical fitness.

• The potential for accidents and the existence of hazards dictate the need for injury prevention. Safe living involves the development and use of safety precautions and the recognition of risk in personal decisions. Injury prevention has personal and social dimensions.

• The use of tobacco increases the risk of illness. Students should understand the influence of short-term social and psychological factors that lead to tobacco use, and the possible long-term detrimental effects of smoking and chewing tobacco.

• Alcohol and other drugs are often abused substances. Such drugs change how the body functions and can lead to addiction.

• Food provides energy and nutrients for growth and development. Nutrition requirements vary with body weight, age, sex, activity, and body functioning.

• Sex drive is a natural human function that requires understanding. Sex is also a prominent means of transmitting diseases. The diseases can be prevented through a variety of precautions.

• Natural environments may contain substances (for example, radon and lead) that are harmful to human beings. Maintaining environmental health involves establishing or monitoring quality standards related to use of soil, water, and air.

Populations, Resources, and Environments

- When an area becomes overpopulated, the environment will become degraded due to the increased use of resources.
- Causes of environmental degradation and resource depletion vary from region to region and from country to country.

Natural Hazards

- Internal and external processes of the earth system cause natural hazards, events that change or destroy human and wildlife habitats, damage property, and harm or kill humans. Natural hazards include earthquakes, landslides, wildfires, volcanic eruptions, floods, storms, and even possible impacts of asteroids.

- Human activities also can induce hazards through resource acquisition, urban growth, land-use decisions, and waste disposal. Such activities can accelerate many natural changes.

- Natural hazards can present personal and societal challenges because misidentifying the change or incorrectly estimating the rate and scale of change may result in either too little attention and significant human costs or too much cost for unneeded preventive measures.

Risks and Benefits

- Risk analysis considers the type of hazard and estimates the number of people who might be exposed and the number likely to suffer consequences. The results are used to determine the options for reducing or eliminating risks.

- Students should understand the risks associated with natural hazards (fires, floods, tornadoes, hurricanes, earthquakes, and volcanic eruptions), chemical hazards (pollutants in air, water, soil, and food), biological hazards (pollen, viruses, bacteria, and parasites), social hazards (occupational safety and transportation), and personal hazards (smoking, dieting, and drinking).

- Individuals can use a systematic approach to thinking critically about risks and benefits. Examples include applying probability estimates to risks and comparing them to estimated personal and social benefits.

- Important personal and social decisions are made based on perceptions of benefits and risks.

Science and Technology in Society

- Science influences society through its knowledge and world view. Scientific knowledge and the procedures used by scientists influence the way many individuals in society think about themselves, others, and the environment. The effect of science on society is neither entirely beneficial nor entirely detrimental.

- Societal challenges often inspire questions for scientific research, and social priorities often influence research priorities through the availability of funding for research.

- Technology influences society through its products and processes. Technology influences the quality of life and the ways people act and interact. Technological changes are often accompanied by social, political, and economic changes that can be beneficial or detrimental to individuals and to society. Social needs, attitudes, and values influence the direction of technological development.

- Science and technology have advanced through contributions of many different people, in different cultures, at different times in history. Science and technology have contributed enormously to economic growth and productivity among societies and groups within societies.

- Scientists and engineers work in many different settings, including colleges and universities, businesses and industries, specific research institutes, and government agencies.

- Scientists and engineers have ethical codes requiring that human subjects involved with research be fully informed about risks and benefits associated with the research before those individuals choose to participate. This ethic extends to potential risks to communities and property. In short, prior knowledge and consent are required for research involving human subjects or potential damage to property.

- Science cannot answer all questions and technology cannot solve all human problems or meet all human needs. Students should understand the difference between scientific and other questions. They should appreciate what science and technology can reasonably contribute to society and what they cannot do. For example, new technologies often will decrease some risks and increase others.

Keeping the Beat & In Rhythm

Teacher Information

**NSTA
Objectives:** Regular exercise is important in the maintenance and improvement of health. The benefits of physical fitness include maintaining healthy weight, having energy and strength for routine activities, good muscle tone, bone strength, strong heart/lung systems, and improved mental health. Personal exercise, especially developing cardiovascular endurance, is the foundation of physical fitness.

**Specific
Objectives:** Determine how exercise affects heart rate.

Compare the resting and recovery heart rates of physically active students with those of inactive students.

Compare the resting and recovery heart rates of male students with those of female students.

**Time
Required for *Keeping the Beat*:** 50 minutes

**Time
Required for *In Rhythm*:** Times will vary depending on the investigation the student chooses. One or two class periods should be enough for most students. You may want to set a time limit on this activity.

**Teaching
Strategies:** Copy the Background Information and student activity pages for Keeping the Beat and In Rhythm. Students should read these and answer the Pre-Lab Questions.

Before the lab, find out whether any student has a medical condition that prevents him or her from taking part in this activity.

Students will need one sheet of graph paper for conclusion question #4 of In Rhythm.

For your own information, ask students how many of them exercise or participate in sports on a regular basis. Make a tally of students who are physically active and another list of those who are more sedentary. Record the names of students in the two groups. This will establish the active and inactive student groups that are needed in Procedure D.

Students should work in pairs. Before the end of the lab, draw the following data tables on the board or copy them onto transparencies. Each student can come to the board or overhead projector and record their data in the Active Category table or in the Inactive Category table. After all findings have been recorded, the class can analyze the results.

As an introductory activity, demonstrate how to determine pulse rate. Show students how to find the pulse in their necks (see Keeping the Beat). Allow them to practice taking their pulse for 15 seconds and multiplying by four to find beats per minute. Caution students not to press too hard against the carotid artery because this could cause fainting.

After students take their pulse using the carotid artery, demonstrate how to determine their pulse in the wrist using the radial artery (see Keeping the Beat). Have students practice this technique as well.

Sample Data Tables. (to draw on the board or copy onto transparencies)

Active Category

Student Names	Ave. Resting (From Data Table 1)	After Exercise (From Data Table 2)	1 min.	2 min.	3 min.	4 min.	5 min.	6 min.	7 min.	8 min.	9 min.	10 min.

Inactive Category

Student Names	Ave. Resting (From Data Table 1)	After Exercise (From Data Table 2)	1 min.	2 min.	3 min.	4 min.	5 min.	6 min.	7 min.	8 min.	9 min.	10 min.

Evaluation Rubrics

Name _____

Grading Rubric for Keeping the Beat

Criteria	Points Possible	Points Awarded
Pre-Lab Questions correct	35	_____
Data Table completed and correct	30	_____
Post-Lab Questions correct	35	_____
Total	100	_____

Name _____

Grading Rubric for In Rhythm

Criteria	Points Possible	Points Awarded
Outlined plan for experiment	25	_____
Carried out procedure for experiment	50	_____
Post-Lab Questions correct	25	_____
Total	100	_____

Keeping the Beat

In Rhythm

Regular exercise is important to the maintenance and improvement of health. The benefits of physical fitness include maintaining a healthy weight, having enough energy to undergo daily activities, developing strong muscles, improving bone strength, increasing strength of heart and lungs, improving flexibility, and improving mental health.

Personal exercise is the key to being physically fit. Through regular exercise, the heart becomes stronger and is able to pump more blood with each beat. The lungs also increase in strength, allowing them to take in more oxygen and release more carbon dioxide with every breath. During exercise the cells of muscles use more oxygen and nutrients than they do at rest. These cell resources must be replenished. Similarly, exercise causes cells to produce more waste that must be removed. The heart responds to these needs by pumping harder. The heart, like other muscles, increases in size and strength when exercised. Over time, as the heart becomes stronger, it can pump blood a great distance with less work. A low pulse rate suggests a very strong heart.

Your heart rate constantly changes. Changes in the environment or changes in your level of activity influence the rhythm of your heart. These changes alter levels of carbon dioxide and oxygen in the blood. Your body tries to keep a normal balance of oxygen and carbon dioxide by altering heart and breathing rate.

You can measure your heart rate by taking your pulse. The heart pumps blood to all portions of the body through blood vessels called arteries. The surge of blood from the heart to the arteries is called *pulse*. You can find your pulse at any location on the body where an artery is close to the body surface and can be pressed against firm tissue. Your pulse rate is the same as your heart rate.

Doctors and nurses often use heart rate and breathing rate as indicators of a patient's health. As a general rule, active individuals have a lower pulse rate than less active people. It is important to realize that heart rate can be influenced by several factors, such as age, sex, health status, psychological state, and body temperature. These factors must be taken into consideration when comparing pulse rates of two people. It is also important to note that some people inherit a tendency to have a high or low pulse.

What is a normal pulse? Most doctors agree that 72 beats per minute is an average pulse. The range of normal can vary a great deal. If you feel that your pulse is too high or too low, you should consult your physician. Veteran marathon runners can have resting pulse rates as low as 40 beats per minute. Usually, these athletes are in excellent health.

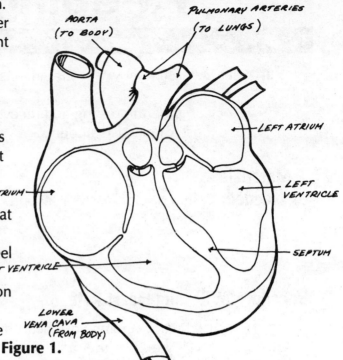

Figure 1.

Since genetics play a role in your pulse rate, recovery rate from exercise is a better indicator of good health than simple pulse rate. *Recovery rate* is the time required for your pulse to return to the resting pulse rate. A quick recovery rate is an indicator of good physical condition.

Pre-Lab Questions

1. Give two reasons why the heart beats more rapidly when you exercise than it does when you rest.

   _____

   _____

2. Define *recovery heart rate.*

   _____

   _____

3. Describe three factors that can influence heart rate.

   _____

   _____

4. Why does exercise make the heart stronger?

   _____

   _____

5. Explain why you can feel a pulse at some locations in your body, but not at others.

   _____

   _____

Keeping the Beat

A Partial Inquiry on Exercise and Pulse Rate

Purpose: Determine how exercise affects heart rate.

Compare the resting and recovery heart rates of physically active students with those of inactive students.

**Materials
Needed:** Watch or clock with a second hand
A chair

Procedure A: Resting Heart Rate

1. Practice finding your heart rate by using either the carotid artery of the neck (Figure 2) or the radial artery of the wrist (see Figure 3).

Figure 2. Take your pulse at the carotid artery. Place the little finger of your right hand on your chin. Drop your middle and index fingers to the side of your neck. Press your fingers lightly against the carotid artery in this location. Do not use your thumb in taking pulse. Do not press firmly against the artery.

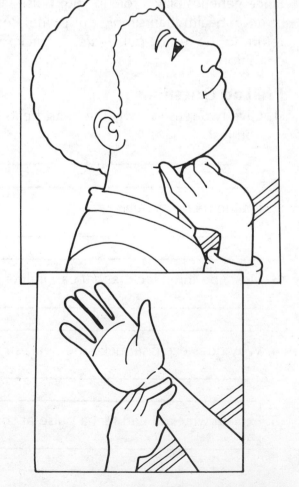

Figure 3. Take your pulse using the radial artery. Use the index and middle fingers to feel for pulse. Do not use the thumb.

2. Heart rate can be measured by counting the pulse. Once you have mastered finding your pulse, you are ready to begin the lab.

3. Sit quietly for two minutes. Your partner will serve as timekeeper and recorder.

4. Locate your pulse and count the number of beats for 15 seconds. Multiply this number by 4 to find heartbeats in one minute. Record this number in Data Table 1 beside "Partner A Resting Heart Rate."

5. Repeat step 4 two more times. Record these numbers in Data Table 1.

6. Add the three entries together and divide the sum by three. This will give the average resting beats per minute. Record this number in Data Table 1.

7. Switch duties with your partner and repeat steps 3-6, recording entries beside "Partner B Resting Heart Rate."

Procedure B: Exercise and Heart Rate

Note: Do not participate in this part of the experiment if you have a physical condition that limits your activity. If you feel faint or dizzy at any time in the activity, sit down immediately and call your teacher.

One partner will serve as timekeeper and recorder as the other partner performs the exercise. Later, roles will switch.

1. Run in place for two minutes.

2. Immediately sit down and find your pulse. Count your pulse for 15 seconds and multiply by 4. Record this number beside "Heart Rate Immediately Following Exercise" under "Partner A" in Data Table 2.

3. Remain seated for the next 10 minutes while you take your pulse at 1-minute intervals. Enter the first number in the "Heart Rate After 1 Minute" row in Data Table 2.

4. After the second minute, take your pulse and enter the number in "Heart Rate After 2 Minutes." Continue in this fashion for 10 minutes.

5. Switch roles with your partner and repeat steps 1-3.

Data Table 1. Resting Heart Rate

Name of Partner A: _____

Name of Partner B: _____

	Trial 1	Trial 2	Trial 3	Average
Partner A Resting Heart Rate				
Partner B Resting Heart Rate				

Data Table 2. Heart Rate (immediately following and up to 10 minutes following exercise)

Name of Partner A: _____

Name of Partner B: _____

	Partner A	Partner B
Heart Rate Immediately Following Exercise		
Heart Rate After 1 Minute		
Heart Rate After 2 Minutes		
Heart Rate After 3 Minutes		
Heart Rate After 4 Minutes		
Heart Rate After 5 Minutes		
Heart Rate After 6 Minutes		
Heart Rate After 7 Minutes		
Heart Rate After 8 Minutes		
Heart Rate After 9 Minutes		
Heart Rate After 10 Minutes		

Procedure C: Rating Yourself

Into which of the following categories do you best fit?

Active: Usually exercise without stopping for at least 30 minutes at a time, at least four times per week. This may include riding bikes, running, walking briskly, jumping rope, playing sports, etc.

Inactive: Usually exercise less than four times per week for 30 minutes

Procedure D: Reporting Your Findings

Go to the chalkboard and record your findings beside your name under the Active or Inactive Category.

Post-Lab Questions

1. How did your average resting heart rate compare to your heart rate immediately after exercise?

   _____

   _____

2. When did your highest heart rate occur?

   _____

   _____

3. Did you ever return to your average resting heart rate after exercise? If so, how many minutes did it take?

   _____

   _____

4. According to the results on the board, compare the resting heart rates of active students with the resting heart rates of inactive students.

   _____

   _____

5. According to the results on the board, compare the recovery heart rates of active students with the recovery rates of inactive students.

   _____

   _____

In Rhythm

A Full Inquiry on Exercise and Pulse Rate

Purpose: Compare the resting and recovery heart rates of active females with the resting and recovery heart rates of active males.

Compare the resting and recovery heart rates of inactive females with the resting and recovery heart rates of inactive males.

Materials Needed: _____

_____

_____

_____

Procedure: Design an experiment in which you compare the resting and recovery heart rates of active males to active females, and of inactive males to inactive females.

Steps in Your Procedure

1. _____

_____

2. _____

_____

3. _____

_____

4. _____

_____

5. _____

_____

Results: Create your own data table if you need one.

_____

_____

_____

Your Data Table

Post-Lab Questions

1. What is the problem that you are trying to solve in this investigation?

_____

_____

_____

2. Explain why it would not be a fair study to compare active females with inactive males. How did you make certain that this did not happen in your experiment?

_____

_____

_____

3. Overall, do males or females tend to have the lower resting heart rates?

_____

_____

_____

4. Draw two line graphs to show a comparison of male and female pulse rates. One graph should compare active males with active females, while the other graph should compare inactive females with inactive males.

Too Many, Too Soon & Don't Crowd Me!

Teacher Information

NSTA
Objectives: When an area becomes overpopulated, the environment will be diminished due to the increased use of resources.

Specific
Objectives: Students raise seeds and fruit flies in populations of various sizes to determine how population size degrades the environment and, therefore, affects the growth rate of individuals and size of the population.

Time
Required for *Too Many, Too Soon*: Day 1—20 minutes
Days 5 to 13—10 minutes
Day 14—30 minutes

Time
Required for *Don't Crowd Me!*: Varies with student designs, but may require parts of three days.

Teaching
Strategies: Copy Background Information and Student Activity pages for students. Have them read the Background Information on Too Many, Too Soon and Don't Crowd Me! and answer the questions.

As an introductory activity, create a circle with a diameter of six feet by drawing a large circle on the floor or by placing desks in a circle. Place a paper plate of inexpensive candy inside the circle. The circle represents an environment and the candy represents its resources. Follow the procedure below to simulate population growth and resource depletion:
   a. Ask two students to enter the circle, take a piece of candy, and eat it.
   b. After the students eat, the population will double to show that populations generally grow exponentially as long as there are plenty of resources. Therefore, ask two more students to enter the circle. All of the students in the circle should eat again.
   c. The population doubles again, so have four more students enter the circle. All of the students eat a piece of candy.

Continue in this fashion until the students are too crowded to fit in the circle, or until the food supply is depleted. Ask them what has happened in this environment? What happens to organisms that do not find any food?

For the partial inquiry, Too Many, Too Soon, prepare a sunny location in your room or some other convenient place where plants can be raised. Radish seeds, grass seeds, or Wisconsin Fast Plants can be used in this lab.

In the full inquiry, Don't Crowd Me!, students raise fruit flies under varying conditions to determine how population size is affected by resource availability. Fruit flies (Drosophilia) are easy to raise in the classroom. Flies, fly medium, and fly anesthesia can be purchased from biological supply companies. Instead of anesthesia, flies can be placed in the freezer for a few minutes. This slows them down so that they can be counted easily.

Evaluation Rubrics

Name _____

Grading Rubric for Too Many, Too Soon

Criteria	Points Possible	Points Awarded
Student grew grass in cups A, B, and C	10	_____
Data Table was complete	20	_____
Graph was complete and drawn in three colors	20	_____
Pre-Lab Questions correct	25	_____
Post-Lab Questions correct	25	_____
Total	100	_____

Name _____

Grading Rubric for Don't Crowd Me!

Criteria	Points Possible	Points Awarded
Outlined plan for conducting experiment	20	_____
Listed materials required for experiment	20	_____
Created a Data Table	20	_____
Created a graph to show growth rate(s) of fruit flies	20	_____
Post-Lab Questions answered correctly	20	_____
Total	100	_____

Too Many, Too Soon
& Don't Crowd Me!

What do you need to live? All living things depend on their environment for everything they require, including food, water, space, and warmth. When a population begins reproducing in an environment where there are plenty of resources, the population grows rapidly.

Think about the life cycle of the common housefly. A month-old female housefly can lay 100 eggs. About half of her eggs are females. Each of these females can also lay 100 eggs within a month. If a female fly lays 100 eggs, and her 50 daughters all lay eggs, and these all lay 100 eggs, the fly population increases dramatically. See Table 1 to follow the size of the fly population over four generations.

Table 1. Growth of Fly Population over Four Generations

Generation	Number of flies in population
1	2
2	100
3	5,000
4	250,000

To see the growth of this fly population graphically, see Figure 1.

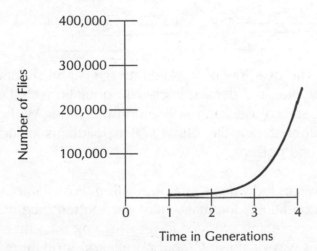

Figure 1.

This incredibly fast population growth is not completely realistic. In life, the natural predators of flies reduce the size of the fly population. Additionally, some of the eggs will not hatch, and others will produce unhealthy individuals. However, as long as there are plenty of resources, fly populations will grow almost as fast as shown in the graph in Figure 1.

The rapid growth of this population can come to a stop if the flies use up one of their resources. For example, if the large population of flies eats all of the food in the environment, the flies will starve. Or, if they use all of the water or oxygen in their environment, their population size will suddenly be reduced.

Large populations lower the quality of their environment. Air and water pollution are some of the problems caused by the world's large human population. Air pollutants include gases produced by cars, factories, and power plants. Some of these gases are the cause of acid rain. Other gases create breathing problems for some people.

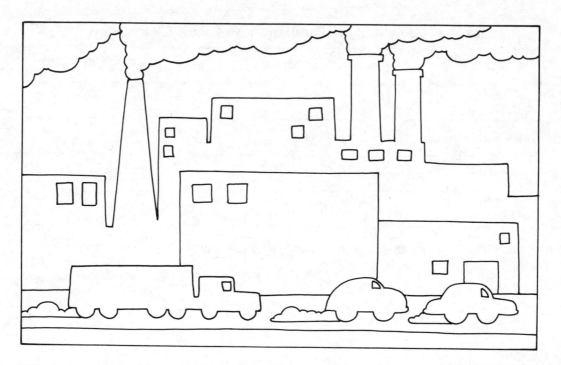

Water pollution is caused by several factors. The overflow of sewage into rivers and streams causes algae to grow rapidly. When this algae dies and decays, bacterial populations that feed on the algae increase. The large number of bacteria use up the oxygen in the water. Without oxygen, the water cannot support fish and other aquatic life. Other water pollutants include oil and gasoline, disease-causing organisms, and poisons.

Overcrowding has negative effects on the lives of individuals in a population. For example, in cages where rats are raised under crowded conditions, the males fight more often than usual. Sometimes the females become temporarily sterile and produce fewer offspring than they normally produce. These changes are nature's way of slowing rapid population growth.

Pre-Lab Questions

1. What are some of the things that organisms require from their environment?

_____

_____

_____

2. If every individual in an environment produces two offspring in its lifetime, how many individuals will be found in the population after ten generations? Complete the following table to calculate your answer.

_____

_____

Generation	Number of individuals
1	2 (1 male and 1 female)
2	4
3	
4	
5	
6	
7	
8	
9	
10	

3. What are some factors that prevent populations from growing very rapidly?

_____

_____

_____

4. How does a rapidly growing population affect its environment?

_____

_____

_____

Too Many, Too Soon

A Partial Inquiry on Overpopulation

Purpose: Raise grass seeds in populations of various sizes to determine how population size degrades the environment and, therefore, affects the growth rate of individuals within that population.

Materials Needed:
Grass seeds
Three small, plastic cups or flower pots
Potting soil
Water
Ruler
Labels

Procedure Day 1:

1. Label three plastic cups as cup A, cup B, and cup C.

2. Fill each cup ⅔ full of potting soil.

3. In cup A, plant 50 grass seeds by spreading the seeds on the soil and stirring them gently with your hand. Do not plant seeds too deeply.

4. In cup B, plant 25 grass seeds.

5. In cup C, plant 5 grass seeds.

6. Water the seeds in each cup with 30 ml of water. Place all three cups in a sunny location. Continue to water the cups each day. Always water them the same amount. The soil in the cups should be moist, but not soaked.

Procedure Day 5:

7. Measure the grass plants emerging from the seeds, average their measurements, and record the averages in the Data Table.

8. Measure these blades of grass daily and enter their lengths in the Data Table. Repeat this procedure daily for two weeks. Each day, also note the color of the grass.

Procedure Day 14:

9. In Graph 1, show the average growth of grass blades in each cup with a line graph. Use red to indicate growth in Cup A, blue to indicate growth in Cup B, and green to indicate growth in Cup C.

Data Table 1. Average Growth of Grass Blades in Cups

	Cup A	Cup B	Cup C
Average Length of Grass Blades in mm/Color of Blades			
Day 5			
Day 6			
Day 7			
Day 8			
Day 9			
Day 10			
Day 11			
Day 12			
Day 13			
Day 14			

Graph 1. Average Growth of Grass Blades in Cups A, B, and C

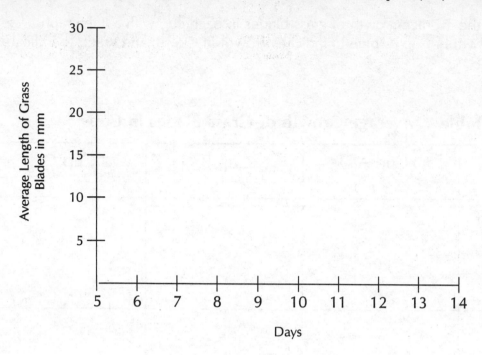

Post-Lab Questions

1. In which cup did the grass seeds produce the longest plants?

_____

_____

2. Did all of the seeds in cup A germinate? in cup B? in cup C?

_____

_____

_____

3. If you decided to extend this experiment for another 30 days, what do you think will happen to the grass seeds in each cup?

_____

_____

_____

Don't Crowd Me!

A Full Inquiry on Overpopulation

Purpose: Raise fruit flies in populations of various sizes to determine how population size degrades the environment and, therefore, affects the growth rate of individuals and size of the population.

Materials Needed: _____
_____
_____
_____

Procedure: Outline your plans for comparing the growth of fruit flies in crowded and in uncrowded conditions.

Steps in Your Procedure

1. _____
_____
2. _____
_____
3. _____
_____
4 _____
_____
5. _____

Results: Create your own data table if you need one.

_____
_____
_____

Your Data Table

Create your own graph to show change in growth of fruit fly populations over time.

Post-Lab Questions

1. What is the purpose of this investigation?

_____

_____

2. What is the control in your experiment?

_____

_____

3. What is the variable in your experiment?

_____

_____

4. If you wanted to raise fruit flies under conditions where you would have maximum population growth, how many flies would you place in a container of food?

_____

_____

HISTORY & NATURE OF SCIENCE

Science as a Human Endeavor
- Women and men of various social and ethnic backgrounds—with diverse interests, talents, qualities, and motivations—engage in the activities of science, engineering, and related fields such as the health professions. Some scientists work in teams, and some work alone, but all communicate extensively with others.

- Science requires different abilities, depending on such factors as the field of study and type of inquiry. Science is very much a human endeavor, and the work of science relies on basic human qualities, such as reasoning, insight, energy, skill, and creativity—as well as on scientific habits of mind, such as intellectual honesty, tolerance of ambiguity, skepticism, and openness to new ideas.

Nature of Science
- Scientists formulate and test their explanations of nature using observation, experiments, and theoretical and mathematical models. Although all scientific ideas are tentative and subject to change and improvement in principle, for most major ideas in science, there is much experimental and observational confirmation. Those ideas are not likely to change greatly in the future. Scientists have changed their ideas about nature as they encounter new experimental evidence that does not match their existing explanations.

- In areas where active research is being pursued and in which there is not a great deal of experimental or observational evidence and understanding, it is normal for scientists to differ with one another about the interpretation of the evidence or theory being considered. Different scientists might publish conflicting experimental results or might draw different conclusions from the same data. Ideally, scientists acknowledge such conflict and work towards finding evidence that will resolve their disagreement.

- It is part of scientific inquiry to evaluate the results of scientific investigations, experiments, observations, theoretical models, and the explanations proposed by other scientists. Evaluation includes reviewing the experimental procedures, examining the evidence, identifying faulty reasoning, pointing out statements that go beyond the evidence, and suggesting alternative explanations for the same observations. Although scientists may disagree about explanations of phenomena, about interpretations of data, or about the value of rival theories, they do agree that questioning, response to criticism, and open communication are integral to the process of science. As scientific knowledge evolves, major disagreements are eventually resolved through such interactions between scientists.

History of Science

• Many individuals have contributed to the traditions of science. Studying some of these individuals provides further understanding of scientific inquiry, science as a human endeavor, the nature of science, and the relationships between science and society.

• In historical perspective, science has been practiced by different individuals in different cultures. In looking at the history of many cultures, one finds that scientists and engineers of high achievement are considered to be among the most valued contributors to their culture.

• Tracing the history of science can show how difficult it was for scientific innovators to break through the accepted ideas of their time to reach the conclusions that we currently take for granted.

Who Were They? & What Do You Think?

Teacher Information

NSTA
Objectives: Individuals and teams have contributed and will continue to contribute to the scientific enterprise.

Specific
Objectives: Students will survey fellow students to determine their interest in science and the extent of their knowledge of historically important scientists.

Time
Required for *Who Were They?*: Day 1—can vary with the size of the survey, at least 30 minutes of class time
Day 2—1 hour

Time
Required for *What Do You Think?*: About 80 minutes; varies according to student designs.

Teaching
Strategies: Copy the Background Information and the student activity pages for students. Also copy the Survey of Contributions of Famous Scientists. Have students read the background information on Who Were They? and What Do You Think?

As an introductory activity, show students pictures of one or two famous scientists. Discuss the contributions of these scientists and the period of time in which they lived. Create a time line of some of the scientists that students know.

In the partial inquiry, Who Were They?, students need to interview other students outside of their science class. Allow them to take their surveys to lunch, recess, and home overnight.

In the full inquiry, What Do You Think?, you might prefer to give different students different assignments, so that students can interview and survey people in their own class. Some other possible survey topics include:
number of science classes that students have attended
number of science-related books that students have read
ability of students to recognize pictures of scientists

student knowledge of present-day scientists
kinds of science that interest students (earth, life, physical, etc)
time of day that students prefer to study science
number of students who plan to study science after high school
survey of general science knowledge

Evaluation Rubrics

Name _____

Grading Rubric for Who Were They?

Criteria	Points Possible	Points Awarded
Pre-Lab Questions correct	25	_____
Included at least 10 students in survey	25	_____
Bar Graph correct	15	_____
Post-Lab Questions 1-5 correct	15	_____
Post-Lab Question 6 correct	10	_____
Post-Lab Question 7 correct	10	_____
Total	100	_____

Name _____

Grading Rubric for What Do You Think?

Criteria	Points Possible	Points Awarded
Listed materials	20	_____
Wrote steps for procedure	20	_____
Wrote and conducted survey	20	_____
Created bar graph to display survey results	20	_____
Post-Lab Questions correct	20	_____
Total	100	_____

Who Were They?

& What Do You Think?

Our present-day, affluent standard of living is due in part to the work of scientists living today and those who have lived in the past. When asked to name some important scientific discoveries, many people begin their lists with space travel. This popular scientific endeavor has placed people on the moon and beyond.

However, there are many great scientific discoveries that have received less publicity than space travel. The materials and conditions that define our everyday life, such as electricity, plumbing, automobiles, stoves, skateboards, and refrigerators, have not always existed on the earth. The technologies that have made these useful objects available were developed through the work of many scientists.

Students are aware of some scientists and their contributions. You can use a survey to determine the scientists that students know the best. In a survey, one gathers existing information and tries to interpret it.

Surveys are useful ways of gathering information from a large group of people. In a good survey, the questions are very clear, so that those reading or hearing the survey know exactly what they are being asked. If you are taking a survey, you must answer questions honestly. There are no "right" or "wrong" answers on surveys. However, dishonest answers give confusing results.

Surveys can be used to find out what people know, or how they feel, on a variety of topics. Politicians survey voters to see what voters think of them. TV viewers are surveyed to determine which programs they watch the most. Food manufacturers survey customers to learn what foods are most popular.

Once a survey is complete, it must be analyzed, and its results organized so that they can be understood by everyone. Data tables, charts, and graphs are a few of the ways to organize the results of a survey. Such visual aids make it easy to understand a survey and its results. (see Figure 1).

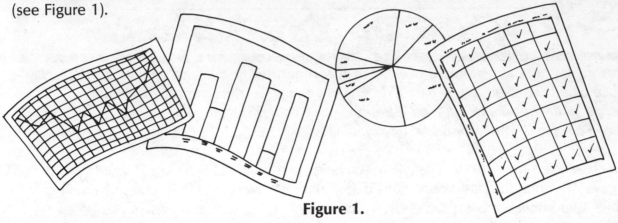

Figure 1.

To be accurate, a survey must include a fairly large number of people. If you survey only two or three people on their favorite TV programs, your results will not necessarily represent the feelings of everyone in the area. Three friends might watch "Lassie" every night because they all love dogs. Their special interest in dogs may not reflect the interests of other community members.

Pre-Lab Questions

1. What are some of the contributions scientists have made to our daily lives?

_____

_____

_____

2. What is the purpose of a survey?

_____

_____

_____

3. How are surveys used in everyday life?

_____

_____

_____

4. What are some ways the information gathered during a survey can be organized or displayed?

_____

_____

_____

Who Were They?

A Partial Inquiry That Surveys Students' Knowledge of Famous Scientists

Purpose: Using a survey, determine whether or not students are aware of the contributions of some historically important scientists.

Materials Needed: Survey of Contributions of Famous Scientists
List of Famous People
Pencil and paper

Procedure: 1. Read the Survey of Contributions of Famous Scientists.

2. Survey at least 20 students. To survey a student:
   • determine whether or not the student has heard others discuss the answers to this survey; if they have, do not use their responses. Their answers would not truly show what they know about scientists who have lived in the past.
   • hand the student the list of scientists and some other famous people. They can choose their responses to survey questions from this list.
   • read the student the survey questions.
   • check their correct responses on the survey form. Give each student up to five minutes to finish the survey.

3. Display your results in a bar graph. Write the names of scientists on the X-axis of the graph, and percentages of students on the Y-axis. Show each scientist in a different color on the graph.

To determine the percentage of students who answered a question correctly, divide the total number of students surveyed into the number who responded correctly to a question. Multiply your answers by 100.

% = <u># of students who responded correctly</u>
     total # of students

List of Famous People

Alexander Graham Bell	Ptolemy
George Washington Carver	Ernest Rutherford
Copernicus	Socrates
William Custer	George Washington
Charles Darwin	Woodrow Wilson
Thomas Edison	Democritus
Albert Einstein	Eli Whitney
Alexander Fleming	Marie Curie
Galileo	Mark Twain
Margaret Mitchell	Sir Isaac Newton

Survey of the Contributions of Famous Scientists

Student Names	Place a check in the box if student gave a correct response to the following questions.				
	Who discovered laws of gravity, inertia, and momentum?	Who said that the characteristics of groups of organisms change over time?	Who discovered penicillin, a drug that kills some bacteria?	Who stated that the earth revolves around the sun, rather than the sun around the earth?	Who explained that energy can be changed into matter with the formula $E = mc^2$?

Bar Graph—Percentage of Students Who Knew Each Scientist

	Newton	Darwin	Fleming	Copernicus	Einstein
100%					
95%					
90%					
85%					
80%					
75%					
70%					
65%					
60%					
55%					
50%					
45%					
40%					
35%					
30%					
25%					
20%					
15%					
10%					
5%					

Correct answers to the survey:

Newton—discovered the laws of gravity, inertia, and momentum.

Darwin—said that the characteristics of large groups of organisms change over time.

Fleming—discovered penicillin, a drug that kills some bacteria.

Copernicus—stated that the earth revolves around the sun, rather than the sun around the earth.

Einstein—explained that energy can be converted into mass with the formula $E = mc^2$.

Post-Lab Questions

1. What are you trying to determine in this investigation?

_____

_____

_____

_____

2. Why is it important that we remember the work of past scientists?

_____

_____

_____

3. According to your results, which scientist is most familiar to students you surveyed?

_____

_____

_____

4. To conduct this survey, you read questions to students and recorded their answers. Suggest another way to conduct a survey.

_____

_____

_____

5. Draw a bar graph that shows the number of males who knew each scientist and the number of females who knew each scientist.

_____

_____

_____

6. In a survey of consumers' favorite cereals, 100 people gave the following answers:

Cereal	% of People Who Chose This as Their Favorite
Goody Grain	25
Raisin, Nut, Banana Bran	50
Cherry Squares	25

Depict the results of the survey by creating a circle graph in the space below.

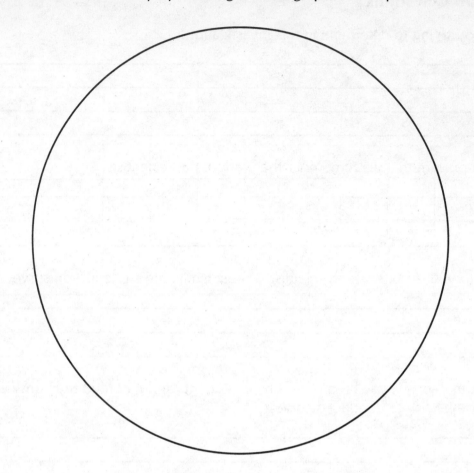

7. Surveys have shown that *Audacious Alice*, a new television show, has been growing in popularity over the last year. Information on its ratings with viewers are shown below. Place this information in the following line graph.

Month	% of Viewers Who Watch *Audacious Alice*
January	17
February	15
March	16
April	19
May	17
June	20
July	21
August	18
September	20
October	20
November	19
December	22

Graph: Percentage of Viewers Who Watched *Audacious Alice* in the Last Year

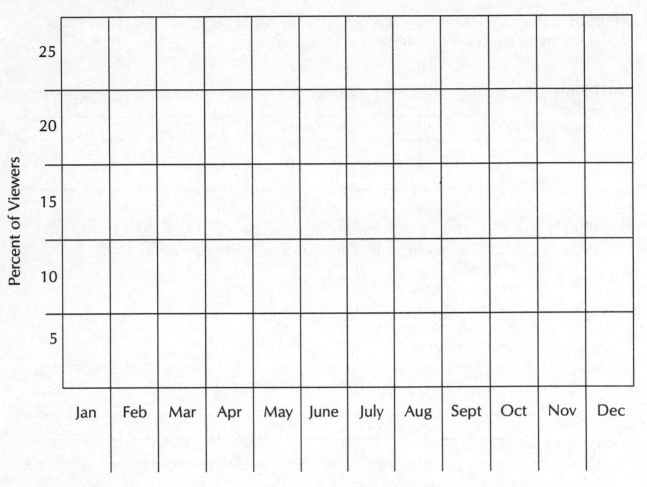

Percent of Viewers

25

20

15

10

5

Jan Feb Mar Apr May June July Aug Sept Oct Nov Dec

Months

What Do You Think?

A Full Inquiry Using a Survey to Compare Male and Female Interest in Science

Purpose: Students will develop and conduct a survey of fellow students to determine how they rank their interest in science.

Materials Needed: _____

_____

_____

_____

Procedure: Design a survey for students to determine how they rank their interest in science. One ranking system that you may choose to use is:

Extremely Interested (5),
Very Interested (4),
Somewhat Interested (3),
Not very interested (2),
Uninterested (1)

Steps in Your Procedure

1. _____

_____

2. _____

_____

3. _____

_____

4. _____

_____

5. _____

_____

Your Survey

_____

_____

_____

_____

_____

_____

Your Data Table

Results: Create your own graph to display your results.

Post-Lab Questions

1. What are you trying to determine in this investigation?

   _____

   _____

2. What are the results of your survey?

   _____

   _____

3. Did you find more males or females who stated that they were "Very Interested" in science?

   _____

   _____

4. What are some factors that could cause your survey to be inaccurate?

   _____

Answer Key

Pre-Lab Questions to Dense Foods   Page 8
1. *Density* is mass per unit volume.
2. Pour it into a graduated cylinder.
3. Find the mass of the liquid, then divide the mass by the volume.
4. six cubic feet
5. 6.6 ml.
6. Physical properties include color, freezing point, boiling point, odor, and state.
7. 2 g/ml

Post-Lab Questions to Dense Foods   Page 10
1. Compressed
2. volume and mass
3. decreasing volume
4. water displacement
5. Answers will vary. A sample answer might be.
   a. Establish the volume of milk with graduated cylinder.
   b. Weigh the cylinder.
   c. Weigh the cylinder and milk.
   d. Subtract to find the weight (mass) of milk.
   e. Divide mass by volume.

Post-Lab Questions to Are You Dense?   Page 12
1. determining the density of copper and comparing the density of the pre-1982 and post-1983 pennies
2. Answers will vary. Probably water displacement, weigh on the scale, and formula would be the general response.
3. Same as number 2.
4. No. Answers will vary.
5. No. Answers will vary.
6. Answers will vary, but most students will conclude that a material cheaper than copper should be used.

Pre-Lab Questions to Feed the Seed and Potash, Anyone?
                                          Page 16
1. Without them, plants develop deficiency diseases.
2. potassium, nitrogen, and phosphorus
3. yellow leaves, leaves that fall off of the plant, scorched leaves
4. state or define the problem
5. State the problem, research it, and form a hypothesis. Without some background information, you cannot make an educated hypothesis. The hypothesis provides you with an idea to test by experimentation.

Post-Lab Questions to Feed the Seed   Page 20
1. how does the amount of nitrogen in a plant's diet affect its growth and appearance
2. The amount of nitrogen is the variable.
3. cup F, no nitrogen
4. Answers will vary, but seeds in cups B, C, and D should grow well.
5. B, C, and D

6. Graph of average seedling growth over 14 days:

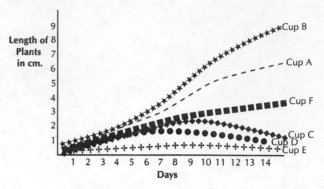

Post-Lab Questions to Potash, Anyone?   Page 23
1. the effect of various potassium levels on plants
2. the amount of potassium given the plants
3. Answers will vary. The control would be the absence of potassium given to plants.
4. Answers will vary. It should be based on the plants that grow best.
5. Answers will vary. Most students will find the plants yellow and lose their leaves.
6. Answers will vary. Most students will find the plants appear wilted.
7. Answers will vary depending on the procedure selected by the student.

Pre-Lab Questions to The Force Is with Us and Speed On
                                          Page 29
1. An object at rest tends to remain at rest, and an object in motion tends to remain in motion, unless acted upon by an outside force.
2. Inertia is an object's resistance to change of position.
3. They change or alter the position of the stationary object.
4. A moving body, such as one in a car, tends to remain in motion.
5. An object at rest is moved by unbalanced forces.

Post-Lab Questions to The Force Is with Us   Page 31
1. Increasing the mass of the force increases the distance that the box moves.
2. It shows a direct relationship between the mass of the force striking the stationary object, and the distance traveled by the stationary object.
3. box
4. The passenger may stumble. The passenger tends to remain at rest when the bus moves forward.

Post-Lab Questions to Speed On!   Page 33
1. How does the speed of a force on a stationary object affect that object?
2. Student answers will vary. They might have simply pushed the weights against the boxes at different speeds.

3. The greater the speed of a force, the more it altered the inertia of the resting object.
4. 55 miles per hour; the greater the speed of a force, the more it alters the inertia of a resting object

Pre-Lab Questions to What's Your Reaction?   Page 37
1. In a chemical change, a new substance is formed. In a physical change, a new substance is not formed.
2. Bubbling and fizzing indicate that a new substance, a gas, has been formed.
3. Change of state, from liquid to vapor, is a physical change.
4. oxygen
5. coat it with a protective metal, such as zinc

Post-Lab Questions to What's Your Reaction?   Page 40
1. test tubes C and D
2. test tubes A and E
3. test tube B
4. Oxygen. Oxygen is required for rusting. Yes. Boiling drives oxygen from the water.
5. Oxygen. Yes. Calcium chloride removes oxygen.
6. Oxygen. Yes. Rusting occurred.
7. Iron and oxygen.
8. A new substance is formed from iron and oxygen.

Post-Lab Questions to Ocean Winds   Page 42
1. In this lab, students are trying to determine what, if any, effect sodium chloride has on the rate of rusting.
2. sodium chloride
3. Student answers may vary. Iron exposed to water, or to air, could serve as a control.
4. Sodium chloride speeds rusting.
5. Iron structures near the ocean rust more quickly than inland structures because they are exposed to salty ocean air.

Pre-Lab Questions for No UV on Me and Stay Cool Page 49
1. Fungi:
   a. cannot make their own food.
   b. cannot move.
   c. have a cell wall.
2. UV radiation is a type of radiation that can be harmful to living things. The sun is the major source.
3. It can cause sunburn, skin cancer, and eye damage.
4. alcohol and bread
5. A cell is the basic unit of life. Cells can carry out all life processes such as absorbing food and water, growing, and reproducing.

Post-Lab Questions for No UV on Me   Page 52
1. How does UV radiation affect yeast cells?
2. the presence of UV radiation
3. beaker A
4. beaker A
5. Answers will vary.

Post-Lab Questions for Stay Cool   Page 54
1. How is yeast growth affected by temperature?
2. temperature
3. room temperature

4. Answers will vary. Yeast usually grows best at room temperature.
5. warm place, away from light
6. slightly warm oven. This provides the best growing conditions.

Pre-Lab Questions to Kitty Cat Genes and Kitty Cat Toes   Page 59
1. A pure dominant has two dominant genes while a hybrid has one dominant and one recessive.
2. two
3. A dominant gene masks the appearance of the recessive gene.
4. No. Both parents possess only recessive genes. Yes. If the black cow and bull are hybrids, they have recessive white genes that can be passed on to offspring.
5. No. They do not have any dominant genes for short hair to pass on to the offspring.

Post-Lab Questions to Kitty Cat Genes   Page 64
1. Answers will vary, but you would expect about 25 to be short-haired and about 25 to be long-haired.
2. The male cat does not possess any dominant genes for short hair to pass on to his offspring.
3. Orange. It masks the black coat color.
4. 100%
5. Student results will vary.

Post-Lab Questions to Kitty Cat Toes   Page 66
1. What percentage of five-toed cats will result from breeding a pure six-toed cat with a hybrid six-toed cat?
2. Answers will vary.
3. none
4. about 10 kittens. About half of the kittens will receive the father's dominant gene for six toes.
5. No

**Pre-Lab Questions to
The Chemical Breakdown of Rocks   Page 74**
1. Weathering is the wearing away and breaking down of rocks.
2. Physical weathering reduces the size of rock particles while chemical weathering changes and the material that composes the rock.
3. The type of rock, minerals that compose the rock, weather, and other environmental conditions all contribute to the degree of rock weathering.
4. Carbonic acid can react with minerals in limestone to dissolve the portions of the limestone. This changes the structural appearance of the cave.
5. The more precipitation in an area, the faster the weathering for rocks made of water-soluble minerals. Weathering also occurs more rapidly in areas where there are drastic temperature differences or high levels of pollutants in the air.
6. Physical. Only particle size, not composition, is changed by the wind.

Data Table. Mass of Beakers and Their Contents

	Mass of beaker and contents at Start	Mass of beaker and contents on Day 2	Mass of beaker and contents on Day 4
Beaker A	620.2 grams	594.5 grams	571.4 grams
Beaker B	652 grams	651 grams	651 grams
Beaker C	631.3 grams	600.2 grams	581 grams

Post-Lab Questions to The Chemical Breakdown of Rocks
Page 78
1. Limestone and marble demonstrate the greatest mass change. Granite changes the least.
2. The lab demonstrated chemical weathering.
3. The mass decreased as time increased.
4. The composition of the rock and the particle sizes were affected.
5. It prevented small pieces of particles from being poured into the sink, but still allowed dirt and water-soluble minerals to be expelled.
6. Granite. A statue made of granite would not be affected by rainfall and acid rain.

Post-Lab Questions to The Physical Breakdown of Rocks
Page 80
1. How physical weathering affects different types of rocks.
2. The type of rock was the variable.
3. Answers will vary according to student procedure. They may choose shaking rocks in containers of water.
4. Answers will vary depending on what rocks were used in the lab. Sandstone is affected more by physical changes than other types of rock.
5. Physical weathering changes only particle size but not composition.
6. The battering of the wind on the sandstone would destroy the structure over time.

Pre-Lab Questions to Water on the Run
Page 84
1. Sand, silt, and clay.
   Sand is the largest. Clay is the smallest.
2. #1 sand, #2 silt, and #3 clay
3. Permeability refers to how well water penetrates the soil.
4. Infiltration is the process of water seeping through pores between soil particles.
5. Material composing the soil, texture of soil, number and size of pore spaces between particles, and how tightly together the particles are packed

Data Table. Time Required for Water to Seep into Soil Particles

	Clay particles (small)	Aquarium gravel (medium)	Marble chips (large)
Time required	Varies, about 5 minutes	Varies, about 40 seconds	Varies, about 5 seconds

Post-Lab Questions to Water on the Run
Page 87
1. sand. clay.
2. clay. Clay's particles are the smallest and they pack closely together.
3. Answers will vary. Clay soil is not very water permeable.
4. clay
5. The larger the particles, the larger the pore spaces in between them. These large pore spaces allow easy penetration by water. This means sand with its large particles would be very permeable to water.
6. Answers will vary, but students should reason that the smaller particles of clay and silt may clog the spaces between the sand and slow water penetration. The time should be much less than that of sand alone, but more than that of pure clay.

Post-Lab Questions to Close Knit
Page 89
1. How pressing soil particles tightly together through packing affects soil permeability.
2. Students should find that the more tightly packed the soil particles, the slower the penetration of water.
3. It reduces it.
4. It packs the soil particles and decreases the pore size between the particles. This reduces the infiltration of water to the plant roots.
5. This prevents soil packing.

Pre-Lab Questions for A Unique Design and My Creative Side
Page 94
1. *Buoyancy* is the upward force exerted by a liquid on an object in that liquid
2. Water level rises. Your body displaces some of the water in the bath tub.
3. salt
4. The hammered steel provides more surface area on which water's buoyant force can act.

Post-Lab Questions for A Unique Design
Page 96
1. Answers will vary.
2. to create a well-thought-out plan before beginning
3. shape one. It exposes more aluminum to the buoyant force of the water.

Post-Lab Questions for My Creative Side
Page 98
1. design and create a product
2. Answers will vary.
3. Answers will vary.
4. Answers will vary.

Pre-Lab Questions for Pretty Bubbles and Oldest Bubbles
Page 102
1. Water, detergent, and glycerine.
2. It reduces water evaporation time in bubbles, extending life span.
3. It reduces surface tension of water.
4. Too much glycerine will prevent bubble formation and too little will not increase life span.

Post-Lab Questions for Pretty Bubbles
Page 105
1. Designing the bubble recipe with the amount of glycerine that makes bubbles last the longest is the problem.

2. The amount of glycerine is the variable.
3. The control is the bubbles made without glycerine.
4. Answers will vary, but one part glycerine to one part soap to six parts water is usually a very effective recipe.
5. Answers will vary. Students should describe how one specific recipe produced long-lasting bubbles.

Post-Lab Questions for Oldest Bubbles   Page 107
1. Answers will vary. Usually one part glycerin to one part soap to six parts water makes long-lasting bubbles.
2. Answers will vary.
3. The amount of soap used in the recipes is the variable.
4. Bubble recipes that do not use soap would be the control.
5. Answers will vary depending on student list.
6. Using a specific bubble recipe, time the life span of bubbles made in warm water versus bubbles made in cold water.
7. Answers will vary, but should promote the recipe students found to produce the longest-lasting bubbles.

Pre-Lab Questions for
Keeping the Beat and In Rhythm   Page 117
1. The heart beats more rapidly during exercise so it can provide the cells with more oxygen and nutrients and also to help rid the body of excess wastes.
2. Recovery heart rate is the period of time after exercise that is required to bring your heart rate back to normal.
3. Heart rate can be influenced by age, sex, health status, psychological state, and body temperature.
4. The heart is a muscle that increases in size and strength when it is exercised.
5. You can find your pulse at any location on the body where an artery is close to the body surface and can be pressed against firm tissue. Other locations may not have arteries close to the body surface.

Post-Lab Questions for Keeping the Beat   Page 122
1. The heart rate increased as a result of exercise.
2. The highest heart rate would occur immediately following your exercise session.
3. Answers will vary depending on the physical conditioning of the student.
4. The average resting heart rates of active students should be lower than those of inactive students.
5. The average recovery heart rates of active students should have been quicker than that of inactive students.

Post-Lab Questions for In Rhythm   Page 124
1. You are comparing the resting and recovery heart rates of males to females.
2. Active individuals will have lower resting and faster recovery heart rates than inactive individuals. To make certain that this did not happen, you should compare the active males to the active females and the inactive males to the inactive females.
3. Males tend to have lower resting heart rates.
4. Answers will vary, but should illustrate overall that a male has a lower resting heart rate and lower recovery time than females of equivalent physical conditioning.

Pre-Lab Questions Too Many, Too Soon   Page 129
1. Answers will vary, but could include food, water, space, warmth.
2. 2828

Generation	Number of individuals
1	2 (1 male and 1 female)
2	4
3	16
4	32
5	64
6	128
7	356
8	712
9	1424
10	2828

3. Answers could vary, but might include lack of food or other resources.
4. It depletes the available resources.

Post-Lab Questions to Too Many, Too Soon   Page 132
1. Answers will vary, but are probably longest in cup A.
2. Answers will vary, but probably answers are yes for cup A, yes for cup B. and no for cup C.
3. Answers will vary, but over time the grass in cup C will become more yellow and show less growth.

Post-Lab Questions to Don't Crowd Me!   Page 134
1. To compare the growth of fruit flies in various population sizes.
2. Answers will vary, but students will probably place 1 to 5 flies in a jar of food as a control.
3. Answers will vary, but students will probably place populations of various sizes in different jars.
4. Answers will vary, but students will probably choose the number in the jar in which fly populations grew the best.

Pre-Lab Questions for Who Are They? and
What Do You Think?   Page 140
1. They have developed products we use daily such as automobiles, stoves, skateboards, refrigerators, etc.
2. Surveys are useful ways of gathering information from large groups of people.
3. Surveys are used to find out what people know or how they feel on a variety of topics. Politicians survey voters about their opinions on topics, TV viewers are surveyed about what shows they like, food manufacturers survey customers to discover their favorite foods.
4. You can organize information from a survey into data tables, charts, and graphs.

Post-Lab Questions for Who Were They? **Page 145**
1. Using a survey, determine whether students are aware of the contributions of historically important scientists.
2. Scientists have given us many contributions that have led to advances in technology. The contributions of past scientists have helped present scientists to add to their knowledge of a topic.
3. Answers will vary.
4. Answers will vary. One possibility is that students could read their own questions and check the appropriate response.
5. Answers will vary based on data.
6.

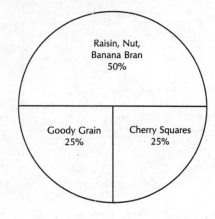

7.

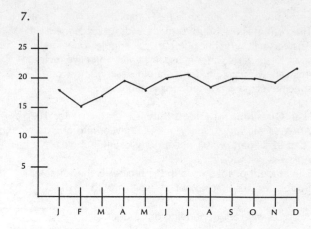

Post-Lab Questions for What Do You Think? **Page 149**
1. Through a survey, students will develop and conduct a survey of fellow students to determine how they rank their interest in science.
2. Answers will vary.
3. Answers will vary. Males tend to be more interested.
4. Answers will vary. Some possibilities include misinformation from participants, the survey administrator gives hints, etc.